More endorsements from Christian leaders

This sixty year perspective from the eyes and heart of Dr. Ted provides not only a "history of the heart," but an insight into God's faithfulness to one of His children. *Reflection on a Pilgrimage* is must reading for those "called to lead" and offers countless examples of servant leadership at its best. Certainly, Ted Engstrom's example should inspire all of us to finish well.

Richard Felix, Ph.D.
President
Azusa Pacific University

Thanks, Ted, for a wealth of information and wisdom that would have been lost if you had failed to step up to the task. All young leaders will benefit from this book. I am forever grateful for Dr. Ted's love and mentorship in my life. This book is not revisionist history; it really happened this way. This is a treasure. Thank you, Ted.

Dr. Jay Kesler
President
Taylor University

Reflections on a Pilgrimage is about faithfulness…the faithfulness of God and the faithfulness of one of His servants. It is the compelling story of one who dared to trust God in all things.

Roger Cross
President
Youth for Christ, USA

Ted Engstrom's book, *Reflections on a Pilgrimage: Six Decades of Service*, is a treasure. It brings a personal perspective to the personalities and ministries of the last 60 years. Beyond that, I was moved by the ministry and influence that Ted Engstrom has had on the evangelical community over his lifetime.

Russ Reid
Chairman
The Russ Reid Company

Reflections is MUST READING for evangelical leaders worldwide. In six succinct chapters reflecting on the last six decades, Ted Engstrom has distilled with great clarity both the culture's societal genre and God's Kingdom momentum. With great global awareness, spiritual insight, personal humor, and strategic analysis, Ted has compiled the most significant defining moments within evangelicalism in the last sixty years. Within each of the six chapters, six leadership credentials of "Dr. Ted" are so evident— an authentic disciple of Jesus; a passionate churchman; a strategic global statesman; an influential mentor; a prolific author; and a true servant leader. I hope that Ted will be able to add several more chapters in the coming decades.

Dr. Gordon E. Kirk
Senior Pastor
Lake Avenue Church, Pasadena, CA

REFLECTIONS ON A PILGRIMAGE

Six Decades of Service

By Ted W. Engstrom

Ted W. Engstrom

(Psalm 32:8)

LOYAL PUBLISHING
www.loyalpublishing.com

Reflections on a Pilgrimage
Copyright © 1999 by Dr. Ted Engstrom
Cover photos copyright © 1999 by Dr. Ted Engstrom
Inside photos copyright © 1999 by World Vision, Inc.
Loyal Publishing, Inc.
P.O. Box 1892, Sisters, OR 97759

ISBN 1-929125-01-1

Printed in the United States of America.

99 00 01 02 03 04 05 06 07 / 10 9 8 7 6 5 4 3 2 1

To Dorthy
Beloved partner for six decades

Table of Contents

Foreword
9

Introduction
13

Chapter 1
The 1940s – The Dynamic Decade
19

Chapter 2
The 1950s – The Fascinating Decade
49

Chapter 3
The 1960s – The Decade of Rebellion
81

Chapter 4
The 1970s – The Decade of Disillusionment
107

Chapter 5
The 1980s – A Decade of Unrest
135

Chapter 6
The 1990s – The 20th Century's Closing Decade
165

FOREWORD

by Dr. James C. Dobson

WHAT A PRIVILEGE IT IS TO WRITE THIS FOREWORD for Dr. Ted Engstrom's new book *Reflections on a Pilgrimage*. He is one of the most influential and respected Christian leaders of our time, having served quietly and often sacrificially in numerous evangelical organizations. Our ministry, Focus on the Family, is blessed to be among them.

I met "Dr. Ted" in 1980 when he was President of World Vision, US. By that time, Focus was only three years old and consisted of about 25 employees. However, our ministry was expanding rapidly which presented us with the challenges of exponential growth. It became obvious that we needed an additional board member who had the managerial experience that the rest of us lacked. Another member, Bobb Biehl, had worked for Dr. Engstrom at World Vision and suggested that I ask him to participate. I wasn't acquainted with him personally but I had heard about his wisdom and dedication to the cause of Christ. Most importantly, he had been where we seemed to be going. Thus, with some apprehension, I approached the busy executive and asked if he would consider joining our board.

Dr. Ted was very gracious, but said that he was already serving on more that 20 boards and really couldn't take on additional responsibility. Besides, he told me with a smile, his wife Dorothy had made it abundantly clear that "enough is enough." I was disappointed but thanked him for his kindness and considered the matter closed. About two weeks later, however, I was asked to show one of the films in my new series to members of the World Vision staff. Dr. Ted was among those present on that afternoon. As we sat in the dark watching a film on fathering, he sent a note down the row that simply read, "I accept your invitation." (Dr. Engstrom recounts this story in the book but remembers writing, "Count me in" on the note.) Either way, the Lord had spoken to him while listening to me talk about my father. It was a divinely appointed moment!

This story illustrates Dr. Engstrom's great heart for Christian ministry. Thousands of others have benefited from his willingness to serve without compensation or reward, except for the knowledge that he was doing the work of the Lord. Dr. Engstrom has now served on our board as vice chairman for 19 years, and in all that time, he has only missed two meetings—both for unavoidable health reasons.

I wish I could explain adequately the enormous contribution Dr. Ted has made to our ministry. Time and again when we were uncertain about the best path to take, he pointed us in the right direction. I'll never forget a board meeting in October 1993, two months after we had completed our new campus in Colorado Springs. Our financial reserved were depleted, and there was reason to believe that contributions during the upcoming Christmas season would be lower than the previous year. One member suggested that we cut millions of dollars from our budget, which would have required the cancellation of numerous successful programs and set the ministry back for years to come. At that point, Dr. Engstrom rose to his feet. (He often stood when he felt strongly about a matter.) For the next few minutes, he made an eloquent and impassioned speech about how the

Lord had taken care of Focus on the Family through the years. We should, he said, continue to trust Him to meet our needs. Then he urged us to press ahead with our original plans. We did, and God did, and the rest is history.

Dr. Engstrom offered similar direction and wisdom to hundreds of other Christian organizations. But his contribution to Christendom has extended far beyond his board service. His great passion continues to focus on needy families, and especially, on the propagation of the gospel of Jesus Christ. His pursuit of those objectives and his effort to ease human suffering has taken him around the world many times.

Reflections on a Pilgrimage presents a fascinating recounting of the experiences and relationships that span this remarkable life. Above all else, Dr. Ted Engstrom is a godly man who has earned the respect of his fellow believers. His accomplishments and Christian service continue to this day, into his eighties. It is my great honor to call him my friend.

James C. Dobson

James C. Dobson, Ph.D.
President
Focus on the Family

INTRODUCTION

The 1940s – The Dynamic Decade

I HAVE BEEN WONDERFULLY BLESSED OF GOD DURING the last six decades to have played a part in the life of the church in this dynamic twentieth century. Gratefully, I have been both an observer and a participant.

The beginning of four distinct careers in my Christian "professional" life began in 1940. Just prior to my first career I graduated from college (Taylor University) in 1938, married my college sweetheart, Dorothy, in 1939, and entered the Christian book publishing field in 1940.

What a ride these six decades have been! In the 40s I served with my close friends, Pat and Bernie Zondervan, first as book editor and then as a manager of the embryonic Zondervan Publishing House, which became one of the premier evangelical book publishers of the nation.

In the 50s and into the 60s I had the privilege of serving first as executive director and then as president of Youth for Christ International in Wheaton, Illinois.

From the mid-60s until I retired in the late 80s, I had the joy and delight of serving in the worldwide ministry of World Vision, headquartered in Monrovia, California, initially as executive vice president and then as president.

And now, as I write this, I am in a fourth, most enjoyable career – consulting with evangelical agencies and leaders (Christian colleges, mission agencies, rescue missions, etc.) along with speaking engagements, writing responsibilities and serving on a dozen or more evangelical boards of directors or trustees.

These have been four paths as led by God: religious book publishing, youth evangelism, world mission activities, and doing my own thing in identification with hosts of meaningful Christian enterprises.

The pages that follow are simply a chronicle of reflections and observations over these sixty years as I have traveled to 136 countries, met and shared with literally thousands of God's choice servants (many of whom I will identify in this book), participated in scores of international conferences and congresses, shared with innumerable churches all across the globe, and met numerous U.S. presidents and heads of state in several nations.

This is in no way an autobiography, albeit it is highly personal, but rather a series of reflections over the years as to God's marvelous working, by His Spirit, in a dramatic, rapidly changing world, society and order.

In Psalm 78:4, the psalmist writes, "We will tell the next generation the praiseworthy deeds of the Lord, His power, and the wonders He has done." This I have sought to do in this book.

As we enter into a new decade, a new century, even a new millennium, perhaps there are some lessons to be learned from the past as to God's working among His people in an ever-changing landscape.

I am most grateful to my colleague and former administrative assistant, George Marhad, presently on the staff of World Vision/U.S. in Seattle, for his wonderful assistance in doing research for me on this project.

And I give God great thanks for being able to witness His working among His people across the globe. I trust you, reader friend, will be encouraged by what you read in these pages, covering six dramatic decades.

"Internationally during this period, over 90 percent of the non-Christian western world came under western domination. The United Nations charter was signed by only 50 nations. After the two atomic bombs were dropped on Japan, the devastating power of the atomic age was unleashed. The world population in 1940 was "merely" 2.5 billion people."

1

REFLECTIONS

The 1940s – The Dynamic Decade

THE DECADE OF THE 40S WAS THE MOST DRAMATIC
and significant decade of the 20th century for the church of Jesus
Christ. This high-octane decade can be divided into two halves—
the first covering World War II, and the second birthing an evangelical resurgence across the nation.

Cost of living (and salaries!) were far lower than today.

In 1940, first class postage was 3 cents (with penny post-
cards); ice cream cones were 5 cents (or a double dip for 10
cents); a loaf of bread was 8 cents; a gallon of gas, 15 cents; a hair-
cut, 50 cents; a visit to the doctor, $2. But the average factory
salary was only $25 a week. (And, our first nice, 3-bedroom
house cost us $7,500!)

An anonymous wag has suggested that in 1940
we didn't have television or penicillin, frozen

foods, Xerox, plastic, contact lenses or frisbees! It
was before credit cards, ballpoint pens, dish-
washers, clothes dryers, electric blankets and air
conditioners. It was a time before daycare centers, group therapy, and nursing homes. We had
never heard of FM radio, tape decks, electric
typewriters, artificial hearts, word processors or
yogurt. It was a time when there were five and
ten cent stores, where we bought things for 5
cents and 10 cents. For a nickel you could ride a
streetcar, make a phone call, buy a Pepsi. We
could buy a new Chevy coupe for $600. Rock
music was Grandma's lullaby and AIDS were
helpers in the principal's office.

Internationally during this period, over 90 percent of the
non-Christian western world came under western domination.
The United Nations charter was signed by only 50 nations. After
the two atomic bombs were dropped on Japan, the devastating
power of the atomic age was unleashed. The world population in
1940 was "merely" 2.5 billion people.

During this period both China and Korea became dominated
by Communist leaders. India and Pakistan became independent,
creating five million refugees. The United Nations partitioned
Palestine into the Jewish and Arab states, and the nation of Israel
was established at the end of the decade, after 1900 years of
being a diaspora nation.

This period saw a technological revolution led by the United
States, Japan and Germany.

The cybernetic revolution began with scientific control of
mechanical, electronic and biological systems and computer
experimentation. This period saw the beginning of what has
become the Information Era, eventually leading to the knowledge worker.

During these war years, shortages and recycling by U.S. citizens were commonplace. Rubber was scarce, gasoline was
rationed (five gallons per week), there were ration stamps for
food, and victory gardens produced a third of what Americans
ate.

Much of the American economy was geared for wartime production, and women entered new fields of the labor force. Seventeen million women were working at one time during the war, representing a third of all workers.

Following World War II we noted Jackie Robinson breaking the racial barrier in major league baseball (1947), the H-bomb was authorized by President Harry Truman, and the first of the baby boomers were born.

Prominent Christian historian George Marsden, writing in the October, 1997 issue of Fuller Seminary's "Theology, News & Notes" had this to say concerning this period of the 40s in America:

> Travel by train was much more common than by plane. Interstate highways were two lanes and most cars were black. The South was solidly Democratic, not quite sure it wanted to be in the Union, and not air conditioned. Most Americans took radical segregation for granted and enjoyed laughing together at *Amos and Andy*. The 'better' neighborhoods and country clubs banned Jews as a matter of course. Asian-Americans were exotic. A woman in a leading profession was a novelty.

> If it is difficult to imagine when all these things were taken for granted, it may be just as difficult for evangelical Christians to imagine what they, or their forebearers, were like in 1947.

> In addition to sharing all the above attitudes, they would have found themselves still very much shaped by the culture of 19th-century revivalism. They were set apart by prohibitions of the classic vices of the bar room and the city: drinking, smoking, dancing, card playing, and theatre or movie attendance. They had built in their own subculture a revival, where they sang the gospel of Ira Sankey, or Fanny J. Crosby, and

learned of their preeminent duty to witness.
They had also been shaped by fundamentalism.
They knew their dispensation charts, and they
opposed Protestant 'modernism.' Like most
Americans they feared Communism and valued
American freedom.

It was into this arena that I stepped to begin my career.

Prior to my conversion to Christ in 1935, it was my goal to become the sports editor of a prominent U.S. daily newspaper. Later the Lord changed that ambition and my desire was to become a part of the Christian book publishing enterprise. Thus, in 1940 I was hired by P.J. and B.D. Zondervan as a book editor at their company, the Zondervan Publishing House, in Grand Rapids, Michigan (at the munificent amount of $30 per week!). It was a decision made never to be regretted. Working in this Christian industry during the action-packed 40s was the greatest possible training and experience I could imagine.

During the next ten years I had the wonderful privilege of meeting and working with some of Gods giants who had books published by Zondervan and with whom I worked as editor.

These included such people as Dr. H.A. Ironside, magnificent pastor of the great Moody Memorial Church in Chicago. He was a transplanted New Zealander who had great gifts as a Bible expositor. Dr. Ironside was the preeminent dispensational spokesman of his day.

Another was Dr. Robert G. Lee, pastor of the Bellevue Baptist Church in Memphis, Tennessee, at that time the largest church in the Southern Baptist Convention. What a spiritual giant he was! His famous sermon, which I helped publish, "Payday, Someday" was preached over 1,000 times by Dr. Lee.

Another friend was Dr. William Culbertson, stately, brilliant president of the Moody Bible Institute of Chicago. In addition there was Dr. Herbert Lockyer, Sr., a prolific British author and Bible teacher who was the first editor of the *Christian Digest* magazine, which I edited for a number of years.

Yet another giant of the faith whom I met and worked with was Dr. A.C. Gaebelein, founder of the Stony Brook School for boys and editor of *Our Hope* magazine. (His son, Frank Gaebelein, also became a well–known and respected friend. Frank was one of the early editors of *Christianity Today* magazine.)

Dr. William Ward Ayer, brilliant pastor of the Calvary Baptist Church in New York City, was also one of the authors I had the privilege of working with. His books sold by the hundreds of thousands.

And let me not forget my special friend Dr. Carl F.H. Henry, eminent theologian, a member of the first faculty at Fuller Theological Seminary. I edited his first book on religious journalism.

The list goes on, but it was a marvelous privilege to work with and know such spiritual giants as these over this significant decade.

One of the unusual assignments I had while serving as book editor was the condensation of the popular four volume set of *The Life of Christ* by F.W. Farrar into one volume. To select only twenty-five percent of the material written about the most important person in human history was a challenge! I also edited a translation from the Danish language of one of Soren Kierkegaard's theological works. (Even today I'm not exactly sure what he said!)

———

Early on in my journalism career, I was inducted into the U.S. Army. My basic training took place at the artillery training center in Fort Sill, Oklahoma. Later I was transferred to a base in Little Rock, Arkansas, then Paris, Texas, and finally to Camp Young in the desert of Southern California where General Patton trained his troops.

On one occasion, while in basic training in Oklahoma and on a twenty-four hour bivouac, I shared an army pup tent with a young fellow soldier, Harry Brooks, whom I had gotten to know quite well. In the dark of the tent that evening, Harry began to ask me a number of questions concerning my Christian faith and what it meant to me. It was a long conversation at the end of which I was able to lead Harry to a saving knowledge of Christ.

Back at the training camp a day or two later, a big, burly trainee from Kentucky stopped me in the latrine one morning and said, "Engstrom, I was in the tent next to you and Brooks the other night and heard your conversation with him about God. I come from a Christian home but certainly am far from God. Can you help me?"

I later shared the Gospel with him, although I don't know whether or not he ever did receive Christ.

I was assigned to a military police unit while in California. On Easter Sunday night in 1944, following duty in Indio, California, where the bars were crowded with drunken soldiers and military people, I was severely injured in a jeep accident on the way back to Camp Young. While unconscious, I was rushed to a military hospital in Palm Springs where it took me about four months to recover.

The experience at the Torney General Hospital in Palm Springs turned into a special gift from the Lord to me. Following my discharge from the hospital, I was assigned to the public relations unit and named editor of the post newspaper, the *Torney Topics*. I edited this publication for over a year, interviewing Hollywood personalities who came to visit our hospital base including Jack Benny, Frank Sinatra and singer Ginny Simms.

More meaningful was the column of spiritual counsel I wrote for each weekly issue, which was seemingly beneficial to our military personnel. In addition, the post chaplain frequently asked me to speak in the weekly chapel services.

While posted at the military hospital, I was invited to give my testimony on the broadcast of the *Old Fashioned Revival Hour* with Dr. Charles E. Fuller, in Long Beach, California. This began a friendship with this giant of the faith.

Dorothy joined me in Palm Springs around then, and was employed in the separation section of the military hospital. As a matter of fact, she signed my separation papers when I was discharged from the Army, and the picture taken of the two of us at the signing was printed in newspapers all across the country.

During this time I had the privilege of helping to establish a military Bible study for the servicemen and their wives stationed in the area. The sobering climate of the world at war heightened the spiritual hunger of hosts of servicemen and women. Close by the military hospital was a U.S. Air Force base. The first sergeant in this unit (the highest ranking noncommissioned officer) and his wife became close friends. First Sergeant Harold and Virginia Carlson from the air base, and Dorothy and I from the military hospital, began a joint Bible study which ultimately was attended by forty or fifty military people on a weekly basis. We formed gospel teams and went to nearby churches on Sunday evenings to conduct evangelistic services.

During this time Harold Carlson and I, together with some of our colleagues, felt led to sponsor a week of evangelistic services for the military personnel around Palm Springs. We asked permission of the pastor of the Community Presbyterian Church, Dr. William McCartney (brother of the famed Pittsburgh pastor, Dr. Clarence Edward McCartney) for the use of the church sanctuary for five nights of meetings. First Sergeant Carlson and I went into Los Angeles on a two-day leave and for those five nights booked five separate speakers: Dr. Charles E. Fuller of the *Old Fashioned Revival Hour*; Louis E. Talbot, president of Biola (Bible Institute of Los Angeles); "First Mate Bob" Meyers, the radio voice of the *Haven of Rest* broadcast; Dr. Don Householder, a prominent Southern California pastor; and Rev. Paul Kenyn, another significant pastor.

As a result of our contact with Dr. Fuller, he invited our Bible study group from the two military bases to periodically hold our meetings in his lovely second home in the Palm Springs area. What a privilege that was for all of us as we got to know Dr. and Mrs. Fuller.

These Palm Springs meetings were promoted widely throughout the area and from the first night on, the church was filled with military personnel—scores of them night by night coming to personal faith in Christ as the message of God's love and forgiveness was proclaimed.

It's interesting to recall that on the closing Friday night, Pastor McCartney asked me if he could share a word with his Palm Springs congregation who were present. (These members had heard of the meetings and, out of curiosity, attended the last couple of nights.) Dr. McCartney told his congregation that he had been their pastor for fourteen years and had never extended a public invitation for folks to come to faith in Christ, but wanted the opportunity to do so that night. A number of civilian adults joined with the military personnel in receiving Christ as Savior in that closing service. I learned an important lesson about offering opportunity to know Christ personally, even at Christian gatherings.

World War II, dating from Pearl Harbor on December 7, 1941, until the peace treaties in Europe and Japan in 1945, was a traumatic, dramatic time for the American populus. Imagine tens of thousands of military personnel being sent out from the churches of America with a great burden of prayer for fellow Christians in the service. The witness of these Christian soldiers, sailors, air force personnel and marines was evident throughout all of the military enterprise. The disruption of the whole world at war created a "go for broke" attitude and spirit of sacrifice among thousands of Christian servicemen and Christian leaders. It also awakened international awareness to replace America's prevalent isolationism.

While in the service for my two–year tour, I continued as editor of *Christian Digest* magazine, which seemed to have a significant impact upon tens of thousands of soldiers who received it from their home churches and families. In each issue I had an article which I entitled "The Adventures of a Christian Soldier." I sensed that these articles had a strong impact upon the lives of those military people who read it, judging by the number of letters received from other military individuals who identified with the challenges of military life as a believer.

This interlude in my publishing career was certainly ordained of God for it gave me a fresh desire to give my life to lay evangelism and instilled in me convictions about the importance of "marketplace" Christians sharing their faith.

In the 40s I was introduced personally to the arena of Christian writing with the Zondervan Corporation. My college major was in journalism and I was eager to pursue that interest.

Early on I was asked to describe the adventure, courage, sacrifice and spiritual depth of several missionaries through a series of brief, paperbound biographies, an assignment I thoroughly enjoyed researching and writing. I was trying to capture in print the inspiration and passion for God and the lost, held by missionaries such as J. Hudson Taylor in China, William Carey in India, Mary Slesser of the Celebes, the martyred John and Betty Stam in China, and Adonirom Judson in Burma.

When the destruction and sacrifice of World War II were finally over, and worldwide totalitarianism defeated, the latter half of the 40s saw a tremendous surge of interest in Christian outreach. The war affected all churches and every assembly of believers.

Between 1940 and 1950, evangelicals founded sixty new Bible colleges to meet the tremendous surge in young people wanting a biblical education. Scores of significant parachurch ministries were begun as the Holy Spirit opened eyes to create ways to reach a lost and hurting world for Christ. This burst of energy also created a more distinct evangelical ministry.

It seemed that a world war not only curtailed America's isolationist tendencies, but God used it to cause much of His church to care for the spiritually lost worldwide.

As an example of evangelical zeal, in the early 1940s many evangelicals felt that certain other Christian groups in America were seeking to monopolize a particular religious viewpoint on radio and in Christian publications. As a result, one of the primary reasons for forming the National Association of Evangelicals in 1942 (and later its affiliate, the National Religious Broadcasters) was to retain the right to disseminate the Gospel and to continue to call people to repentance, personal faith in Christ and into involvement in Christian missions.

During this decade, even our most prominent political leaders sensed the importance of biblical faith and values, and that America could win a war but lose its soul.

In 1946 President Harry Truman told a group of churchmen that "without a moral and spiritual awakening" America would be lost. General Dwight D. Eisenhower echoed this, suggesting that there was no hope of avoiding a disaster "except through moral regeneration." Likewise, General Douglas MacArthur invited missionary agencies to send 10,000 missionaries to Japan to "provide the surest foundation for the firm establishment of democracy." Most regrettably this did not happen in a large scale fashion and a great opportunity was lost.

During the war and in the tension-filled years following, Americans seemed more hungry for spirituality than they had for decades. In this changed climate, evangelicals found that their calls for religious and moral revival fell on sympathetic ears. I had the privilege of witnessing the birth of a host of these significant ministries, and sharing in their development. America's "can do" optimistic spirit found fresh expression among evangelicals directly following the war.

It was while I was editorial director at Zondervan, following my service in the military, that I was asked to become director on a volunteer basis of the burgeoning new Youth for Christ movement in my hometown of Grand Rapids, Michigan. This position led to my first meeting with evangelist Billy Graham.

Graham graduated from Wheaton College in 1944, and during the last year of his college career he pastored a church in Western Springs, Illinois, near the campus. Two years following his graduation he became the first full-time employee of the newly-founded Youth for Christ movement, based in Chicago. He joined them as an evangelist.

The Christian Businessman's Committee (CBMC) in Grand Rapids was the sponsoring agency for the Youth for Christ program which I directed in that city. We agreed together that it would be great to invite this dynamic preacher to come to Grand Rapids for a five-day evangelistic campaign (later to be called Crusades). I was asked to lead these meetings.

For this young journalist it was an unforgettable experience. It was Graham's first city-wide evangelistic campaign—to be followed by literally hundreds of such Crusades to reach urban masses over the ensuing years. A neutral, popular site was selected, and the Grand Rapids Civic Auditorium, seating 5,500 people, was filled night after night with young people coming to faith in Christ. That was the start of a warm personal relationship with this godly individual.

In the years following, Billy Graham was a guest in our home and I, in turn, was a guest with him in his parents' home in

Charlotte, North Carolina. (More about Dr. Graham in subsequent chapters.)

The last half of the decade of the 40s saw the birth of literally scores of strong, evangelical parachurch ministries. God had prepared thousands of young men and women to leave their small ambitions and extend the reach of the Church. Tens of thousands of others sacrificially prayed and gave encouragement. Included were: Young Life, The Navigators, Youth for Christ (YFC), Fuller Theological Seminary, *The Word of Life* program led by Jack Wyrtzen, the Far East Broadcasting Company, Gospel Films, Inc., Mission Aviation Fellowship, The Moody Institute of Science, The National Association of Evangelicals (NAE), The National Religious Broadcasters, and a host of others.

Dick Hillis was a missionary to China who was evacuated with other missionaries in 1949. Dick helped start the large Los Angeles Youth for Christ rally and later began to minister to Chinese exiles in Taiwan, (then known as Formosa). This was the beginning of a mission that became known as Overseas Crusades.

About the same time Paul Freed, Director of the Greensboro, North Carolina, YFC rally, established Transworld Radio as a result of his post-war overseas preaching tours. The organization set up headquarters in Monte Carlo.

In addition Robert (Bob) Evans, a former Navy chaplain who had been wounded in the Normandy campaign, became YFC International's first executive director upon his discharge from the military. Evans led an evangelistic team in Europe soon after the war. He was drawn to the educational needs of young European converts and founded the European Bible Institute near Paris early in the 1950s, which eventually developed into the fine missionary society known as the Greater Europe Mission.

In reflecting back, it is both encouraging and humbling to me to note that I was involved in some way or another with each of these very special ministries and their founders, for which I praise God.

Following the war, in city after city, born again men and women were forming Fisherman's Clubs, Breakfast Clubs, Christian Business Women's Councils, and the Christian Businessmen's Committees.

These groups functioned both as channels for fellowship and discussion about ethics in the workplace, as well as seeking as their mandate the sponsoring of evangelistic projects. Bringing in newcomers and having them exposed to the Gospel was their primary stated purpose.

The CBMC committees grew at an explosive rate during the 1940s. There were seventy-five committees reported in operation in 1944 and 162 by 1947. These groups took on increasingly ambitious evangelistic projects, expanding from their customary lunch break service in downtown theatres to sponsoring weekly radio broadcasts, youth rallies and servicemen's centers during the war. By the mid 1940s, the CMBMs were beginning to organize citywide evangelistic crusades, the scale of which had not been seen since Billy Sunday was at his peak earlier in the century. A grass-roots lay movement was turning the allegiance of tens of thousands of urban dwellers to Christ.

Some of the key names that surfaced in this period of time included the fascinating Miss Henrietta Mears, director of Christian education at the First Presbyterian Church of Hollywood. This dynamic woman, often called "Teacher," deeply influenced scores of young men who, because of her inspiration and guidance, entered Christian ministry and made a significant impact upon the Church. This list included Bill Bright, Richard Halverson, Louis Evans, Jr., and hosts of other Christian leaders. She was also the founder of Gospel Light Press, writing and publishing helpful material for Sunday school teachers.

During this time of critical outreach to young people, the InterVarsity Christian Fellowship (IVCF) launched its Urbana Missions Conference at the University of Illinois, beginning with 500 or 600 in attendance and ultimately challenging 20,000 students in its triennial conferences to give their lives for the lost and unreached of the world.

Simultaneously, in Dallas, seminary student Jim Rayburn began the significant evangelistic ministry to high schoolers, which he called Young Life.

Effective evangelistic outreach in changing times required sound theological thinking. During the 40s this led Dr. Harold Ockenga, pastor of Boston's famed Park Street Church (for over thirty years) to also become the first president of Fuller Theological Seminary (for eleven years), commuting between Boston and Pasadena. Later he was also chairman of the board of *Christianity Today* and was an early pioneer with the National Association of Evangelicals and The World Evangelical Fellowship.

As evangelicals presented Christ as the answer to human needs, they increasingly felt a demand for strong biblical and theological teaching. This teaching was provided by several superb leaders. Dr. Lewis Sperry Chafer was the widely appreciated president of Dallas Seminary. In the same city Dr. W. A. Criswell became the pastor of the Dallas First Baptist Church with, at that time, 10,000 members.

Dr. Wilbur M. Smith was recognized as a preeminent Bible teacher, teaching first at the Moody Bible Institute, then serving as professor of English Bible at Fuller Seminary.

Dr. Carl F. H. Henry's scholarly contribution in the area of theology, teaching at Fuller Seminary and then becoming editor of *Christianity Today* magazine, also began in the 1940s.

Another dear friend, Dr. V. Raymond Edman, a former missionary to Ecuador with the Christian and Missionary Alliance, assumed the Wheaton College presidency in 1940. He was an avid promoter of missions and missionary spirituality. He frequently used episodes from the life of J. Hudson Taylor, founder of the China Inland Mission, in his chapel talks, and he personally counseled students in their pursuit of the surrendered life. The link between Christ-centered living and effective witness was clearly emphasized.

Hosts of other significant personalities surfaced on the church scene during this time, most with whom I had at least an acquaintance if not a special friendship. These included radio broadcaster and pastor Dr. J. Vernon McGee, Theodore Epp of the *Back to the Bible* broadcast, Peter Dyneka of the Slovic Gospel Association, W. Cameron Townsend, founder of the Wycliffe Bible Translators, Samuel M. Shumaker, prominent Episcopalian pastor and author in Pittsburgh, Dr. Samuel M. Zwemer, seminary professor and evangelist to the Muslim world, Senate chaplain Peter Marshall, Lutheran prayer advocate, Armin Gesswein, and so many others who made a significant impact on the American church landscape during these years.

As America had focused on winning a war in 1942, two New England evangelical leaders, Dr. J. Elwin Wright, Director of the New England Fellowship, and Dr. Harold Ockenga, pastor of Boston's Park Street Congregational Church, felt called to bring together other leaders in the evangelical world to a special gathering to be held in St. Louis. The burden was to share mutual concerns regarding the evangelical witness across a troubled nation. Approximately 150 invited guests came to this conference and formed what became know as the National Association of Evangelicals (NAE).

The NAE had a tremendous influence upon its membership, as it either founded or inspired a variety of ventures including the National Religious Broadcasters, the Evangelical Theological Society, the Evangelical Press Association and the Evangelical Foreign Missions Association (EFMA). The NAE was a great confidence builder, proving that wonderful innovations could emerge from collective effort. Evangelicalism's message of personal faith in Christ and the authority of the Bible now had a stronger voice through these collaborative alliances.

A second conference was called for the following year, in 1943, and I had the privilege of attending that conference held in Chicago representing Zondervan. Approximately 350 delegates gathered from all across the country, representing thirty-four denominations, and were wonderfully bonded together in the task of uniting evangelicals nationwide. For me, it was an unforgettable experience, as the Holy Spirit began to break down distrust and unhealthy individualism, and showed us the power of unity under Christ's Lordship.

At the Chicago conference, Harold Ockenga was elected as the first president, and Free Methodist Bishop Leslie Marston became the first vice president. Herbert J. Taylor of Chicago, president of the Club Aluminum, was selected to be the treasurer. The conference closed with a strong address by the Southern Baptist spellbinder, Dr. Robert G. Lee of Memphis.

I will never forget the experience of being with strong, godly personalities facing enormous challenges with a determination to reach a confused, searching nation with the Gospel of Christ. Clearly, certain personalities stood out among us as noteworthy.

Seated in the auditorium one day with a friend, we noticed a tall, handsome young man walking down the aisle. My friend said to me, "Watch that young man. He's a comer!"

I asked who he was. My friend replied, "That's Torry Johnson, pastor of the Midwest Bible Church here in the city. Mark my words, he's going to make a name for himself!" Indeed he did— as the founding president of Youth for Christ, making the name of Christ dearly loved among tens of thousands of youth.

In those days, no ministry made a greater impact upon me than that of Youth for Christ. It soon became synonymous with lively Saturday nights—for the glory of God!

During the days of the war, a number of Saturday night Youth Rallies began to spring up simultaneously in various parts of the country—in Indianapolis as led by Roger Malsbary, in Detroit with Ed Darling, in Minneapolis with George Wilson, in Los Angeles with David Morken, in Washington, D.C. with Glenn Wagner, in St. Louis with Richard Harvey, in Boston with John Huffman, and in Chicago with Torrey Johnson. It was a phenomenon that captured the imagination of church and lay leaders across the nation. Teens were looking for purpose, fun, excitement and challenges and the Saturday night rallies were geared to these young people—especially to those in the military. The meetings were lively, with upbeat music, skits, youth testimonies and always a strong Gospel message.

In 1944 Torrey Johnson, then pastor of the Midwest Bible Church in Chicago, and director of the Chicagoland Youth for Christ program, called together those individuals who were leading these rallies to meet at the Christian conference grounds in Winona Lake, Indiana as the guest of the conference director, Dr. Arthur McKee. At this week long conference, a charter was drafted and a constitution developed, officially organizing what became Youth for Christ International.

In the years immediately following, literally hundreds of communities—large and small—began YFC programs, led by dedicated volunteer individuals determined to not neglect the teens in their communities. I was among these volunteers who, beginning in the winter of 1945, led the program in Grand Rapids, Michigan.

In the earlier rallies across the country led by Torrey Johnson, frequent speakers included individuals such as Freelin Carlton, manager of the large Sears Roebuck department store in Chicago, Herbert Taylor, president of Chicago's Club Aluminum, and R.G. LeTourneau, earth moving manufacturer from Peoria.

The group held a second annual convention in the summer of 1946 at Medicine Lake, Minnesota, and I was invited to attend. What a privilege it was to meet these enthusiastic, energetic, godly young leaders who gathered together to share their experiences and to strategize regarding the future of this new organization. The conference was led by Torrey Johnson as president, and included Billy Graham, Bob Cook, Cy Jackson, Charles Templeton, Bob Pierce, Hubert Mitchell, George Wilson, Waiter Smyth and scores of other committed youth leaders and evangelists. Being with these godly young men, and seeing their determination to reach unchurched youth for Christ, made an indelible impression upon my life and experience. (It was following this time in Minnesota that we determined to invite young evangelist Billy Graham to our Grand Rapids community.)

At the third annual YFC conference in Winona Lake in 1947 plans were consummated for a World Congress on Evangelism to be held in Switzerland the following year. I was invited to this Congress as a delegate and asked to take on the responsibilities of handling press relations for the conclave, sending out daily news releases to the religious press across the nation and elsewhere in the world from which these delegates had come. Russell Hitt, editor of *Eternity* magazine, was my associate in this responsibility.

The vision for this conference came upon thirty-seven year old YFC president Torrey Johnson as he was traveling in Europe during the summer of 1947. He had seen postwar Europe at its worst and his heart was burdened. He later testified that God was talking to him and had given him this idea—not for himself or for Youth for Christ, but for all who wanted the world reached with the Gospel.

At that summer Winona Lake Convention, the organization adopted a staggering $538,000 budget (enormous for that time) for 1947-48, with $340,000 of it earmarked for overseas use.

Billy Graham came to Grand Rapids once again in 1948 for a special outdoor rally at a baseball stadium at which time he raised the funds for me to attend this European meeting, which was called the Beatenburg Conference.

An evangelical Bible school high in the Swiss Alps at a place called Beatenburg, overlooking the Sea of Thun, was selected as the venue for the conference. Over 450 delegates from more than thirty-five nations around the world came to the Conference where we witnessed an amazing outpouring of the Spirit of God upon us. It was, for me, a defining moment in my life as I was challenged with and burdened by the need for world evangelization. It was at that conference that I committed my life to the task of evangelization, leaving smaller ambitions behind.

A host of significant pastors, missionaries and Christian leaders addressed the conference. Included were people like Billy Graham, Torrey Johnson, Bob Cook and the famed missionary pastor from the People's Church in Toronto, Dr. Oswald J. Smith.

I vividly recall Dr. Smith's challenge to us regarding an agency such as Youth for Christ. He indicated that in his judgment, ministries always began with a man, soon became a movement, then degenerated into a machine and ultimately became a monument. He warned us—and others—to be careful to keep the fire burning in our hearts. He was the one who asked the question, "Why should anyone hear the Gospel over and again when most of the world has yet to hear it the first time?"

Some of the delegates who attended this conference included evangelist Merv Rosell, Evon Hedley, Phil and Louis Palermo, well known musician/evangelists, Bob Evans, Roy McKeown, Harold Ockenga, and numerous American YFC leaders. From overseas came such individuals as Canon Tom Livermore of Great Britain, evangelist Boris Bessmertny from France, Peter Schneider of the YMCA in devastated Berlin, Max Atienza and

Greg Tingsen from the Philippines, along with hosts of others who were making their mark for God in various parts of the world.

On my way to the Beatenburg Conference I spent a couple of days in London visiting with the leadership of a sister Christian publishing firm to Zondervan known as Marshall, Morgan and Scott. The managing director, Mr. James Cook, was my host for those days. It was most interesting to see the effects of the World War II bombings, which had just ceased a relatively short time before my visit in 1948. The ravages of war were still everywhere in the heart of that city.

Following the conference, and some ministries in the South of France and Italy with some of my Youth for Christ colleagues, I flew to Amsterdam and was present for the opening sessions of the first gathering of the World Council of Churches at the famed ConcertGebau Hall. Church leaders—both conservative and liberal—met together to form the WCC.

On the flight to Amsterdam our pilot circled the city of Rotterdam and indicated that for the first time since the war the lights of the city were lit. Quite excitedly he shared the fact that he was seeing these lights himself for the first time. It was quite a moving experience for all of us on the flight.

After the Beatenburg Conference I returned to my responsibilities at the Zondervan Publishing House, but instinctively felt that God possibly had other plans for me in the years ahead. They were to take shape and form in the next decade of the 1950s.

From this Conference sprung other international mission agencies, including the formation of the Greater Europe Mission, as headed up by Bob Evans, and World Vision, founded by Bob Pierce.

A wonderful sister organization to YFC, founded a bit earlier, is Young Life. Jim Rayburn, a young Presbyterian youth leader in

Texas, started a weekly Bible club for about ten fellows and girls in his hometown. There was singing, a skit or two and an inspirational talk about Jesus Christ. Club attendance jumped dramatically when the group started to meet in the homes of the young people. (Indeed, the Young Life movement became an important model for the entire Youth for Christ ministry.)

Following graduation from Dallas Seminary, Jim and four other seminarians collaborated on the vision God had given them concerning His love for America's lost youth, and Young Life was officially born in 1941 with the establishing of a board of trustees.

By 1946 Young Life moved to a new headquarters in Colorado Springs, Colorado, with a staff of twenty men and women across several states. They initiated creative camping programs in Texas and Colorado. Over the years, tens of thousands of campers have shared in mountain climbing, sailing—and experienced the love of Christ—at a summer, winter or weekend camp.

One of the youth ministries which had a strong influence was Percy Crawford's *Young People's Church of the Air* based in Philadelphia. Crawford was a hard-driving preacher and entrepreneur, born in Canada. He held weekly rallies at Philadelphia's First Presbyterian Church, drawing hundreds of young people. Crawford loved sporty clothes, practical jokes and fast cars. His program moved at a rapid speed as well, and featured trumpet trios, vocal soloists such as George Beverly Shea and Percy's rapid-fire messages.

One of Crawford's proteges was Jack Wyrtzen, a Brooklyn insurance agent who also led a twelve piece dance band. After Wyrtzen's girlfriend and future wife, Marge Smith, was converted at Crawford's Pinebrook Conference, Wyrtzen and his friends were marvelously converted and formed a traveling evangelistic team.

Wyrtzen and his *Word of Life* program in Times Square, New York City, sponsored a Victory Rally on April 1, 1944, in the middle of the war when 20,000 people filled the Madison Square Garden. A year later, Memorial Day, 1945, a rally of Chicagoland Youth for Christ at Soldier's Field attracted 70,000 people, largely teenagers. This rally was addressed by radio broadcaster

Charles E. Fuller. The Chicago *Daily News* proclaimed that Chicagoland Youth for Christ was the "biggest sensation in the world of religious revivals since the day of Billy Sunday."

——— ——— ———

Mission Aviation Fellowship (MAF), originally known as the Christian Airmen's Missionary Fellowship (CAMF), was founded in New York City during the middle of the war years by three young pilots who joined together for prayer, Bible study and the discussion of missionary aviation possibilities. The three men were Jim Truxton, Jim Buyers, and Clarence Soderberg, all seeking to use their unique aviation skills in the cause of world evangelization.

After listening to a missions challenge to the students at the Providence Bible Institute in Rhode Island, Navy pilot Jim Truxton was moved to establish a missionary aviation organization that would operate as soon as World War II concluded.

It was at the 1944 evangelistic rally in Times Square that Jack Wyrtzen's Word of Life Fellowship made the first public announcement concerning the formation of this group. Later that year Dawson Trotman, founder of the Navigators, offered MAF free office space and a part-time secretary in his Hope Street headquarters building in Los Angeles. Betty Greene, serving the office as secretary/treasurer, had the distinction of being the first MAF pilot to fly to and on the mission field.

The inaugural MAF flight took off from a newly bulldozed field at the Lockman Ranch in La Habra, California, in early 1945. Piloting a 1933 Waco biplane, Betty Greene flew two Wycliffe workers to Mexico City and then flew Cameron Townsend, founder of the Wycliffe Bible Translators, to their jungle camp in the state of Chiapas, Mexico. Betty was a model to men and women alike of the courage, risk taking and adventure found in serving Christ in missions.

——— ——— ———

As hard as it may be to imagine today, the premiere radio broadcast in the 1940s was the *Old Fashioned Revival Hour*, founded by Dr. Charles E. Fuller, who was the preaching voice of the broadcast. Fuller was a businessman with little theological training but a passion for evangelism.

He was the son of a prosperous orange grower in Southern California and a graduate of nearby Pomona College. His wife and broadcast partner, Grace Fuller, was the cultured, college educated daughter of a physician. After a short stint as a mining engineer in northern California, Charles settled in Orange County south of Los Angeles, joined a local fertilizing firm, and eventually became a dealer in orange groves and other real estate.

His weekly Sunday afternoon evangelistic radio program was broadcast from the 5,000-seat Municipal Auditorium in Long Beach. The program was marked by great hymns sung by a fine volunteer choir led by H. Leeland Green, a song or two from the Old Fashioned Revival Hour Quartet (formerly known as The Goose Creek Gospel Quartet), the piano artistry of the popular Rudy Atwood, and letters from listeners read by Grace Fuller as she was introduced by Dr. Fuller saying, "Go ahead, honey."

The quartet's smooth renditions of old–fashioned gospel hymns and Rudy Atwood's bright and lively keyboard embell-ishments added a hint of contemporary styling to the program. During the 40s it had an estimated audience of fifteen to twenty million people, the largest audience in national network radio.

From the initial single-station broadcast at KNX in Los Angeles, the program rapidly expanded, reaching practically every metropolitan area in the country. Dr. Fuller himself would lead the audience in singing the chorus the broadcast made famous, "Heavenly Sunshine:"

> "Heavenly Sunshine, Heavenly Sunshine
> Flooding my soul with glory divine
> Heavenly Sunshine, Heavenly Sunshine
> Hallelujah Jesus is mine."

The broadcast was the most appreciated radio program in its time over a thirty-year period. Its quality, popularity and clear Gospel message set a new standard for Christian communicators

using the airwaves across America and beyond. It was my privilege as a soldier to give my testimony on one of the broadcasts.

In this 40s decade, my friends Bob Bowman and John Broger
answered God's call on their lives to broadcast the Gospel to
China by means of shortwave radio. Together they formed the Far
East Broadcasting Company (FEBC) in December of 1945 as an
interdenominational, international Christian broadcast ministry.

They had planned to broadcast from inside China, but
FEBC's application for a broadcast license was denied as the
Communists began forcing missionaries out of that country. As a
result, FEBC established its first broadcast facility in the
Philippines in 1948. The ministry grew rapidly in influence, size
and impact. Many nations restrict Christian activity, but Gospel
broadcasts can soar over the heads of authorities who fear their
influence, and can reach directly into the homes of people who
long to hear the truth.

I had the privilege of visiting the home of Bob and Eleanor
Bowman and the FEBC offices in Manila, and was tremendously
impressed with the pioneering spirit of these gifted and dedicated friends.

The impact of this ministry begun in the 40s continues on
strongly to this day. Currently, broadcasts are heard over most of
Asia and much of Africa, crossing cultural, political and geo-
graphic borders with the Gospel. Programs are sent in more than
150 languages to areas where two thirds of the world's people
live.

The Fuller Theological Seminary, named after Charles E.
Fuller's father, had its roots in the 1940s. Fuller was not content
with "just" his weekly radio broadcast, and his burden to see
theologically trained evangelists and Christian workers led to
the formation of the Fuller Theological Seminary in Pasadena,
California.

In the summer of 1944, the first step was taken toward launching what was initially called the Fuller Seminary of Missions and Evangelism. The Fuller Evangelistic Association had bought a piece of property to the north of the California Institute of Technology in Pasadena. Cal Tech had been using this property for military research and it was hoped that it could be zoned for a graduate school. However, after the war, neighbors would not approve a zone variance. The Fuller Evangelistic Association sold this property and procured a five–acre plot of ground very close to the Pasadena Civic Center and only a block from the main library. It was the largest piece of unused property in the center of the city.

Prior to building on this property, the seminary had a temporary location where it could hold classes before its scheduled opening in the fall of 1945. This was at Lake Avenue Congregational Church in Pasadena, which permitted the seminary classes to meet in its three story educational building.

Dr. Fuller invited Dr. Harold J. Ockenga, who had been pastor for ten years at the historic Park Street Congregational Church in Boston, to consider heading up the school as its initial president. Following a considerable number of weeks in prayer and seeking the mind of the Lord, Dr. Ockenga agreed to serve as acting president, commuting on a monthly basis from his Boston responsibilities.

An initial board was comprised of Dr. Ockenga, Mr. Herbert Taylor of Chicago, Dr. Rudolph Logefeil of Minneapolis and Arnold Grunigen of San Francisco.

Several men were approached to serve as the first faculty, including Dr. Wilbur M. Smith, professor of English Bible at the Moody Bible Institute and editor of the annually-published *Peloubets' Select Notes on the International Sunday School Lessons*: Dr. Carl F.H. Henry, professor of theology and philosophy at Northern Baptist Seminary; Dr. Everett F. Harrison, professor of New Testament at Dallas Seminary; and Dr. Harold Lindsell, professor of missions and church history at Northern Baptist seminary. Carl Henry served as dean for the first year and Harold Lindsell as the organizing registrar.

The first class of fifty students, all men, began their studies following an opening convocation at the Pasadena Civic Auditorium in October of 1947 with over 1,500 in attendance.

Obviously, since the 1940s and beyond, the Fuller Seminary has made a remarkable impact upon the evangelical world, both locally and internationally. Ultimately three schools were formed: the School of Theology, the School of World Missions, and the School of Psychology. (More about these in subsequent decades.)

——— ——— ———

Shortly after our marriage and our move to Grand Rapids, Dorothy was invited to participate in the newly founded *Children's Bible Hour* broadcast. This program was the dream of Dr. David Otis Fuller, pastor of the large Wealthy Street Baptist Church in Grand Rapids, and was launched in 1942 over radio station WLAV in Grand Rapids. Mel Johnson, director of the Mel Trotter Rescue Mission in the city, was the show's first director and was known as "Uncle Mel." Three other individuals joined Mel in forming the CBH Quartet which sang on each broadcast. These were Carl J. Bihl ("Uncle Kelly"), Malcolm Cronk, pastor of the large Calvary Church in Grand Rapids ("Uncle Mac") and Morrey Carlson of the Youth Haven Camp in Muskegon ("Uncle Morrey"). Johnny Hallett, well known gospel pianist, was the accompanist.

Our friend Dorothy Boli interviewed youngsters on the air and my Dorothy wrote and told the Bible story each Saturday morning. Children sang in their chorus and many shared in vocal solos and instrumentals. One of these was a young girl, Charlotte Larson, who had a lovely contralto voice. She later married Warren Bolthouse who subsequently became founder and director of the Christian Family Network headquartered in Tucson, Arizona.

The program was eventually heard over scores of stations across the nation and continues on to this day. Dorothy had to leave the broadcast to join me at the military hospital in California after my accident in 1944, but was a part of the program for its initial two years.

——— ——— ———

The last year of the 40s marked the launching of Billy Graham's nationally recognized evangelistic crusades with the memorable ten week event held in a large tent in downtown Los Angeles. It was during this 1949 gathering that newspaper publisher William Randolph Hearst sent word out to his editors to "puff Graham." As a result, reports of this significant evangelistic endeavor hit the pages almost daily in newspapers across the nation.

Numbers of widely recognized personalities were attracted to this crusade and many of them made professions of faith, including such people as songwriter and cowboy singer Stuart Hamlin, former Mafia wiretapper Jim Vaus, and Olympic track star Louis Zamperini. Even Mickey Cohen, the infamous gangster and racketeer, was influenced by Graham and the crusade. These appearances launched Dr. Graham nationally and internationally and as newscaster Paul Harvey says, "Now you know the rest of the story!"

In the mid 1940s my friend Ken Anderson, a popular author with whom I worked at Zondervan, had a burden for producing sixteen-millimeter films for young people. He asked a few of his friends from Michigan to join with him in forming a small board to support this venture which we named Gospel Films. Several of us met together around Ken's kitchen table in Muskegon, Michigan, one Saturday evening to brainstorm what could happen with this vision. These included businessmen Jack Sonneveldt, Charles Peterman, Morrey Carlson and Ted Essenberg, plus Ken Anderson and myself. I was priviliged to serve as first chairman of the company, and Ken as our first president.

From this faint beginning came one of the premiere Christian movie production organizations—and later a producer of video programming—whose films have had tens of thousands of showings in churches, conferences and schools worldwide.The five of us were reminded that "little is much when God is in it." (Ken Anderson later formed a sister film organization, Ken Anderson Films, and was succeeded as president at Gospel Films by Billy Zeoli, director of the Youth for Christ ministry in Indianapolis.)

While in Grand Rapids, I had the privilege of sharing in the founding of the Grand Rapids School of the Bible and Music (GRSMB). Malcolm Cronk, pastor of Calvary Church in Grand Rapids, had a burden for a school to train up Christian workers—primarily for missionary service and music directors for local churches. Joining with us during its first year was Don DeVos, a Moody Bible Institute graduate with unusual musical skills, and John Miles, a fellow classmate at Taylor University and pastor of a church south of Grand Rapids. He became our first president.

The initial class, beginning in 1947, had about thirty–five students and over the years hundreds of these choice young people have been trained and ministered across the world from what was then known as GRSBM (later to be named Cornerstone College).

During our years in Grand Rapids we were active in the Evangelical Swedish Covenant Church. It was interesting to learn that my paternal grandfather was a brick mason and helped to build the church where we worshipped. I had the privilege of leading the youth group in the church and also served as Sunday school superintendent for a number of years.

For two years my close friend and associate, Jack Sonneveldt, and I conducted a 10 P.M. Sunday radio broadcast which we called *The Goodnight Hour*. Jack emceed the program and played his baritone horn and I gave the brief message. It was a youth broadcast and we had young people from the church who gave their testimonies. Obviously, it was an unsophisticated broadcast but one that all of our young people enjoyed every Sunday night.

One of the greatest gifts God gave to Dorothy and me during this period of time was the adoption of our two wonderful sons, Gordon and Don. Both of them came into our home from situations in Grand Rapids and they, together with their adopted sister JoAnn, who joined us as an infant a few years later, have brought joy and delight to us over all of these years. Now they have established their families, with our five grandchildren and two great-grandsons, and bring great delight to our hearts and lives as parents and grandparents.

"The 1950s marked an unprecedented surge in the number of North American missionaries stationed worldwide. The missionary population nearly doubled from 15,000 in 1951 to 27,000 by 1955. A growing remnant of Christians with a worldwide vision were sacrificially dedicating their lives to communicate Christ's love in tangible ways and to planting the Church among unreached peoples."

2

REFLECTIONS

The 1950s – The Fascinating Decade

THE DECADE OF THE 1950S—MID-CENTURY—WAS in sharp contrast to the 40s. We experienced a strong economy, a sense of stability in Washington and unusual growth in the evangelical Church.

However, it was also a period of unrest, with the fear of atomic warfare and the devastating war in Korea (backed by the United Nations Security Council) in the first three years of the period. There were 54,000 Americans killed plus millions of Chinese and Koreans who died in the conflict. Looming large was the international Cold War between communism and capitalism, totalitarianism and democracy.

In contrast to the 40s, the average income increased to $5,600 per year, an automobile cost $1,800, gas prices went up to 26 cents a gallon. This decade saw the beginning of fast–food restaurants, transcontinental air travel, suburban housing tracts growing rapidly, a $1 per hour minimum wage, the launching of the Elvis Presley era, the nightly newscasts of Huntley and Brinkley, and Americans enjoying the situation comedies of *I Love Lucy* and *The Honeymooners*.

The decade marked the first World Series no-hitter by Don Larson in 1956 and the famous three-run homer by Bobby Thompson in the bottom of the ninth for the Giants to win the pennant in 1951.

The hydrogen bomb was introduced in 1952, followed by color TV, the introduction of Xerox copy machines, the launching of the first 707 jets and the introduction of the Salk vaccine against polio.

Popular General MacArthur was removed by President Truman from the Korean command. Senator Joe McCarthy over-stepped his authority, and was censured after anti-communism abuses. World War II hero Dwight Eisenhower was our president for the eight–year period.

Church leaders expressed great concern by many over the national moral decline. Dr. Carl F.H. Henry wrote in the early part of the decade that educators were largely to blame for teaching "ethical relativism." A 1952 issue of *Moody Monthly* magazine warned of the dangers of Christians improperly watching TV as merely a substitute for going to improper movies. Missionaries returning from China reported "wholesale execution of Chinese Christians" in many parts of that nation. Noted historian Kenneth Scott Latourette published his significant *History of Christianity* in 1956.

In 1952 the Lutheran Church invested $750,000 to develop twenty-six thirty minute TV programs titled *This is Life* to portray "typical Christianity in an average American home." This demonstrated part of the creative witness energy coming from many Christian circles at that time. Also in 1952, the American Bible Society claimed that the Bible, or portions of it, was now in 1,049 languages and dialects.

That same year the *Lutheran Hour* radio broadcast celebrated its twentieth anniversary. Worldwide, it was heard on 1,150 stations in fifty-six languages with the popular Oswald Hoffman as the voice of the program.

In the 1952 presidential election, both Adlai Stevenson and Dwight Eisenhower declared their dependence on God and the necessity of strong Christian faith to carry on the historic purpose of the U.S., our government and life.

Racism was a growing issue in the early 1950s. It was during this period that the Supreme Court passed down its landmark decision related to non-segregated schools in 1954. Protest marches all across the South marked these turbulent years.

One year earlier, in 1951, one of the most significant Christian ministries of the last half of the twentieth century arrived on the scene—Campus Crusade for Christ. My beloved friend Bill Bright gave up a successful business career as he saw the urgent need to present the Gospel on American college campuses.

Bill began his ministry at University of California Los Angeles, where he and his wife Vonette lived. In Crusade's first year on the campus, over 250 students accepted Christ and six joined the embryonic Campus Crusade staff. Five years later there were sixty-seven staff members with ministries on fifty college and university campuses. Bill indicated that over three million Americans and 50,000 international students at that time were studying on 2,500 college campuses in the U.S., but less than 5 percent had any active relationship with Jesus Christ and His Church. He felt that the college campus was the most strategic mission field in the world. Campus Crusade ministries spread to some of the most prestigious secular campuses in America, including Harvard, Princeton, Darmouth and Yale.

Early on in the formative years of Campus Crusade, Bill invited me to spend a few days with him at a Crusade staff conference in Mound, Minnesota. It was a memorable and defining moment in discerning God's call on my life. Bill shared his dream of "world evangelization in our generation" with his prime emphasis at that time on college campuses. I shared with him my vision and dream of reaching a generation of high school teenagers with the Gospel. As we prayed together, jointly strategized and compared notes, it was for me one of those key benchmark encounters which cement friendships and determine directions.

The first edition of *Christianity Today* magazine appeared on October 15, 1956. From the outset, this publication has had a tremendous influence upon evangelical thought throughout the last half of the twentieth century. In the opening editorial the editors indicated that the publication had its origin in a deep-felt desire to express historical Christianity to the present generation. It stated that neglected, slighted, misrepresented evangelical Christianity needed a clear voice to speak with conviction and love, and to state its true position and its relevance to the world crisis.

The editors were confident that the answer to the theological confusion existing in the world at that time was to be found in Christ and in the Scriptures. They indicated that through the pages of this new publication evangelical scholars would expound and defend the basic truths of the Christian faith in terms of relevant scholarship and a practical application to the needs of that generation. They declared that the editorial policy of *CT* would unreservedly accept the complete reliability and authority of the written Word of God.

From the very beginning, this magazine—founded by Billy Graham and edited by Carl F.H. Henry, along with Graham's father-in-law, Dr. Nelson Bell—profoundly influenced evangelicals to think far more deeply about the impact the Gospel should have personally and corporately on them and in the world.

The National Association of Evangelicals (NAE) continued to provide points of contact for united action and influence through the evangelical community in the decade of the 50s. The leadership relied heavily upon various service commissions and affiliated agencies, which served a constituency much larger than the official NAE membership.

Besides the national headquarters in Wheaton, Illinois, the movement operated a public affairs office in Washington, D.C., under the direction of my friend Dr. Clyde Taylor, a publications office in Cincinnati, and regional offices throughout the country.

Related organizations were the National Association of Christian Schools, the Evangelical Foreign Missions Association (EFMA), The National Religious Broadcasters, the National Sunday School Association, Evangelical Youth, Inc., and commissions on education, evangelism and church extension, government chaplaincies, international relations, a layman's council, a purchasing agent, a women's fellowship, World Relief, and a Spiritual Life Commission. All of these efforts used NAE influence to enlarge the evangelical center of the Protestant scene.

Many of the 150 evangelical leaders who signed the first official call for the organizing conference in St. Louis in 1942 were still active in the 50s in NAE leadership and its affiliated organizations. Dr. George Ford became the first executive director of NAE beginning early in the decade.

The 1950s marked an unprecedented surge in the number of North American missionaries stationed worldwide. The missionary population nearly doubled from 15,000 in 1951 to 27,000 by 1955. A growing remnant of Christians with a worldwide vision were sacrificially dedicating their lives to communicate Christ's love in tangible ways and to planting the Church among unreached peoples.

It was during this period that the report came of the slaying of the five young missionaries in Ecuador by the Auca Indian tribe. The five missionaries were Jim Elliott, Nate Saint, Ed McCulley, Roger Youderian, and Pete Fleming. The entire Christian world was shocked by the ruthless murder of these stalwart young men on the shores of the Curaray River.

When Jesus prayed to His Father in John 17, He asked for protection for those whom the Father had given Him. For what purpose? "…that they may be one as we are." Protection from what? "That thou should keep them from the evil one." And in Betty Elliott's words, "Protection from disobedience from God's call on their lives."

Each of the five men, years before, had asked for the whole accomplishment of God's will in him at any cost, to the end that Christ Jesus be glorified. God had answered the prayer of His Son and the prayer of the men themselves, as well as the prayer of their wives. These men loved God above all else.

Few events in modern Christian history have influenced the Church more than these five gifted young missionary martyrs. Their deaths made a gigantic impact on much of the evangelical community due to the touching story of courage and pain, primarily for five widows and their children. The first Auca Indian convert was a woman named Dayuma, led to Christ by Rachel, the widow of Nate Saint, who later was baptized by Dr. Raymond Edman, president of Wheaton College.

In baptizing Dayuma, Dr. Edman said, "The Aucas of the Ecuadorian jungles are the most savage and brutal people in the world. The martyrdom of five young missionaries seeking to reach them is the most stirring missionary account of this century. The courageous return of Dayuma, the Christian Auca, to her people, which made possible the going of Rachel Saint, Betty Elliott and her little Valerie to the Aucas, is the greatest adventure in this missionary epic."

The words from Jim Elliott's diary will linger for generations: "He is no fool who gives what he cannot keep, to gain what he cannot lose."

Early in the decade of the 1950s, while I was directing the local Grand Rapids Youth for Christ program as a volunteer alongside my responsibilities at the Zondervan Publishing House, we invited YFC International president Torrey Johnson to Grand Rapids for a fund–raising banquet. He came, and it was a most successful occasion. We were able to raise most of the budget for the ensuing year, with 400 or 500 of our friends present to underwrite the program.

Following the banquet, Torrey invited me up to his hotel room for a time of fellowship.

"Ted," Torrey said, "Bob Cook needs you at the YFC headquarters office in Chicago!" (Bob was Torrey's successor as president of Youth for Christ and, incidentally, Torrey's brother-in-law.) "I'm going to call him right now."

"Don't do it, Torrey," I responded, "I am well positioned in the publishing business and have no desire at all to leave. I feel I'm in this role at the publishing house for a long haul."

Torrey didn't listen! He called Bob at midnight and said, "Bob, I think I have your man for you."

"Torrey, don't do this to me!" He wasn't to be deterred and said, handing the phone to me, "Here, talk to Bob."

Reluctantly, I greeted my friend and told him how amazed I was at this particular phone call. I had known Bob from earlier days so it was not a matter of our getting acquainted.

Bob asked me if I would be willing to go down to Chicago and meet with him and a few of his board members simply to explore the possibility. I demurred at first, but finally said, "Okay, I'll do it, but please don't have any expectations of my leaving Grand Rapids."

A few weeks later I did go to Chicago and met with Bob and three or four of his board members in his office. Among those present I recall were Ed Darling, director of the Detroit program, Dr. Frank Phillips from Portland, secretary of the board George Wilson from Minneapolis, and Dr. Paul Maddox, former Chief of Chaplains of the U.S. Forces in Europe and at that time executive director of YFCI.

The first thing Bob said was, "Guys, let's pray," which we did. Following this time of prayer Bob said, "I don't feel like we really have gotten through, so let's pray some more"—which was a surprise to me. We did so a second time.

A third time Bob said, "There is a spiritual principle that I believe in, and that's 'praying through.'" That was a new experience for me. We prayed again, and in a very strange and wondrous way the Holy Spirit spoke to my heart and indicated that it was important for me to explore this possibility of joining with Bob in the leadership of this new organization.

Returning home, and sharing with Dorothy this invitation, I felt at liberty to ask my special friends and colleagues, Pat and Bernie Zondervan, for a leave of absence, thinking that undoubtedly I would come back after a period of a year or two. They kindly granted my request and I went to Chicago to the office, moved my family to Wheaton, and began my responsibilities as the executive director of Youth for Christ International.

So began the second part of my career path, which lasted for twelve years, never leading back to the publishing business.

Incidentally, both Pat and Bernie Zondervan remained very dear and choice friends of mine. In my leaving, there was no rupture of fellowship. As a matter of fact, many years later Mary Zondervan, Pat's wife, asked me to conduct his memorial service after he went home to be with the Lord.

The 1950s was a decidedly defining period in my life and ministry. Over those ten years I witnessed a stream of miracles by God's grace and working of the Holy Spirit in the YFC ministry.

In taking the post of executive director, which I originally thought would be for a rather short period of time, I experienced what was for me both exhilarating and often times exhausting years of rich blessing and spiritual growth.

It was in 1957 that my predecessor as president of YFCI, Dr. Bob Cook, resigned from the leadership to take a new assignment as vice president of Scripture Press Publishers in Wheaton—and later to become President of King's College in New York State.

The board of directors very graciously invited me to succeed Bob as the third president of Youth for Christ International. It was with fear, trembling and trepidation that I accepted the responsibility to lead this rapidly growing ministry across the world.

A few days after accepting the task, I left for Copenhagen, Denmark, to meet with my old college classmate Sam Wolgemuth, who was doing preparatory work for a YFC Youth Congress to be held in that city. When I told him of my accepting this new assignment, he responded with great shock! We learned to work quite well together, however, and he proved to be a valued colleague in the ensuing years as our vice president for international activities.

From the very beginning of my tenure with Youth for Christ, I was privileged to share in literally hundreds of Saturday night YFC rallies, conferences, and various evangelistic events all across the U.S. and Canada. Reflecting back it seems that I was in practically every U.S. metropolis in that twelve–year span, from Portland, Oregon, to Portland, Maine, and from Minneapolis to Miami.

Some of the outstanding metropolitan area rally services in which I shared come to mind: Chicago, Indianapolis, Memphis, Seattle, Portland, Los Angeles, San Diego, Cleveland, San Antonio, Oklahoma City, Jackson, Mississippi, Philadelphia, Toronto, Winnipeg, Detroit, Des Moines, St. Louis, Kansas City, Phoenix, Denver, Milwaukee, St. Petersburg, Cincinnati, plus hosts of smaller communities.

Each summer I shared in numerous youth conferences—in addition to the gigantic Winona Lake, Indiana, Annual Convention—in such places as Ocean City, New Jersey and Medicine Lake, Minnesota.

One of the great joys and delights on reflecting back on these hundreds of meetings with literally hundreds of thousands of teenagers is to recognize how mightily the Lord worked in winning to Himself tens of thousands of these young people, so many of whom have over the years gone into Christian ministries. In subsequent decades I have met literally scores of these converts all across the globe who are either in Christian ministry or as salt and light in a wide range of professions.

The 1950s in Youth for Christ was marked by several international youth congresses conducted across the globe. My first major assignment as executive director was to set up a Youth Congress in Belfast, North Ireland. This was a new experience for me, i.e. doing set-up work with national leaders, church leaders and others in that North Ireland capital. My new friend, the Honorable Major Ivan Neill, Minister of Labor for the government, and an outstanding Christian layman, was the chairman of our conference planning committee.

I made two trips to Ireland prior to the summer conference, one of which was in the middle of the winter. I gained a new appreciation for the phrase, "bone-chilling cold." The hotel in which I was staying did not have central heating and for the three or four nights that I slept there I had to cover myself with three or four blankets just to gain a little warmth! Strange, how memories of extreme weather stay with you.

Another large Youth Congress on Evangelism was held in Tokyo in 1953, with over 800 delegates coming from across Asia and North America. We met in a large downtown conference center in a city that was still suffering from the ravages of the war which the Japanese people lost. We felt that it was a time of great healing as we were able to minister with our Japanese Christian friends during those days.

Sam Wolgemuth was the coordinator for the Congress, working with David Morken and other Youth for Christ personnel who were ministering in Japan and other parts of Asia.

Following the Congress, twenty-five or thirty separate teams, of three, four or five people on each team, went out to as many cities to conduct evangelistic rallies, particularly for young people. The Spirit of God was pored out upon these teams and hosts of Japanese youths and old alike, came to faith in Christ as a result of the evangelistic outreach.

During this time, teens throughout Europe and Latin America expressed tremendous hunger for Christ. I was privileged to share in the leadership of numerous YFC Congresses in Bristol, England; Caracas, Venezuela; Sao Paulo, Brazil; Copenhagen, Denmark; Madras, India; Mexico City, and the international centers helping to motivate and steer the energy, creativity and Christ-likeness of thousands of young Christian leaders in reaching unsaved teens. Each of these had a different flavor and emphasis, and each had its share of challenges, but each proved to be a powerful ministry to teens to help them find Christ and God's call on their lives.

It was a personal delight to have my oldest son, Gordon, share with our team in the Mexico City Congress. It really was the only time I was able to take any of my children along on an overseas trip, and I know this was a very meaningful experience to Gordon.

A fun-packed, battery-charging highlight each July for YFC staff was the high-energy, inspirational annual Youth for Christ Convention held at Winona Lake, Indiana. The convention was two weeks in length, with a separate group of young people and youth leaders coming each of the two weeks.

It is difficult to describe the Holy excitement that surrounded those fourteen days—with contests, Bible Club meetings, evening evangelistic rallies, great music and a continual sense of God's presence. In many ways, the core values and foundational stories of Christ-centered youth ministry were being informally passed on to a growing cadre of youth workers.

Top speakers were brought in from across the nation to address the thousands of teenagers in attendance at the great Billy Sunday Tabernacle night by night. For each morning of the week we would invite a Bible teacher to address the young people in a series of Bible messages.

A highlight each year was the five-person Bible Quiz Teams from various rally centers across the nation who competed against each other in the exhilarating Bible quiz contests, conducted by Jack Hamilton, Bill Eakin, and members of the high school Bible Club staffs.

In addition, each week there were talent contests for musicians and what were known as "preacher boy" contests. Some of the strongest messages one could hear came from these young men who preached their well-prepared messages.

Convention business was conducted each year including the election of the officers, the establishing of a budget and forming together the vision for ministry in the year to follow.

One night in each of the two weeks we would call for a late night prayer session held in the auditorium of the Free Methodist Church up the hill from the conference grounds. We would begin the prayer session at about 10:30 or 11 P.M. and rarely would conclude it before daybreak. These became unforgettable experiences as hundreds of us met together to pray, seeking God's face for direction for the ministry among the millions of teenagers across the nation and around the world. People like Armin Gesswein and Peter Deyenka led these meaningful prayer sessions.

Peter, founder of the Slavic Gospel Association, was a Russian with a strong accent who prayed in a loud voice which could be heard literally a block away. One night following one of his prayers, another man in the prayer meeting said, "Peter, you know the Lord isn't deaf, don't you?"

"Yes, I know," Peter responded in fun, "and He's not nervous either!"

Some residents at the Winona Lake Conference Center were particular friends and patrons of Youth for Christ. One of these was Mrs. Billy "Ma" Sunday, wife of the famed evangelist. She had a lovely home on the hillside by the lake and year by year would invite our leadership team up for tea in her home. I recall that this widow, well-positioned financially, would come to have meals with us in the hotel dining room on occasion and at the conclusion of the luncheon or dinner would pick up some of the rolls that we had not eaten, wrap them in a napkin and take them home with her!

Another special friend who lived at Winona Lake was Homer Rodeheaver, the famed song leader in the Billy Sunday campaigns. He and his sister Ruth Thomas had a lovely home at Rainbow Point and they too would annually invite our leadership team there for a special post-evening rally buffet.

There were always two services held each evening—the first an outdoor service in what was called the Hillside, was broadcast over Chicago's Moody Bible Institute radio station WMBI each evening from 6:30 until 7:30 P.M.. This service was largely music, with testimonies from the young people themselves, and then a brief word from one of our staff members. This Hillside broadcast was heard all over the Midwest and the response indicated that it was one of the most popular features on the WMBI schedule of programming.

In a survey conducted nationwide at about the time of our Winona Lake Convention, it was indicated that the most popular religious song was "The Old Rugged Cross." One night we had the privilege of having the writer of this great hymn with us, Mr. George Bennard. He was interviewed by one of our vice presidents, Roy McKeown, and indicated to the teenagers how the writing of this great gospel song came about. It was a most moving experience for all to hear this gentle, white-haired song writer share his testimony.

Keeping on top of the finances for Youth for Christ International—salaries, mortgage payments, overhead, etc.— was a constant challenge for us, as with almost all non-profit organizations.

Each year for several years in the 50s we had a mid-winter conference for our donors and supporters at a lovely Boca Raton, Florida, Bible Conference grounds. One evening we invited some of our friends to join with us in a late evening prayer meeting at which time we expressed our concern over our finances and asked our friends to pray with us concerning the supply of our needs.

A young man was in the group by the name of Bruce Bell. He indicated to my colleague Evon Hedley and me following the prayer time that his father was the head of the Glenmede Trust in Philadelphia, which handled the funds for the Pew Memorial Trust. This Foundation was funded by Mr. J. Howard Pew, a prominent Presbyterian layman who was the chairman of the Sun Oil Company. Bruce told us that perhaps his father could be of help to us if we laid our needs before him.

I commissioned Evon to go to Philadelphia to meet the father, Mr. Allyn Bell, as his son had suggested and lay the burden before him for our financial needs. Some weeks later, during another prayer meeting at a church near our offices in Wheaton, there was a phone call from our friend Mr. Bell, indicating that they were putting in the mail that day a substantial check to meet those pressing needs, which included meeting our payroll the following day.

The Pew Foundation was one of several key generous foundations which assisted us financially over the years, including the Lilly Endowment Fund in Indianapolis, the Crowell Trust in Chicago and the Kresge Foundation in Detroit. In addition, there were a large number of corporate entities, headed up by Christians, who generously gave on an annual basis to the ministry as well. I'm convinced that God will not forget their faithful, visionary giving, and I have always been deeply thankful for their heart for young people.

Highlights in this period of the history of Youth for Christ included Capital Teen Conventions held in Washington, D.C., in late Decembers between Christmas and New Year's. Each time, 10,000 teenagers from YFC programs across the nation gathered for four days in the nation's capital for a time of challenge to be Christ's witnesses on their high school campuses. The young people came from every part of the country and returned to their communities with a new zeal in their witness for the Savior. Top–notch speakers and musicians provided the challenging program for these choice young men and women.

Roy McKeown, director of the Los Angeles YFC program and our national YFC vice president, was the director of the conventions, assisted by Jack Daniels from our headquarters office. God was doing a new thing in the hearts of hundreds of thousands of America's teens, and we had the privilege of urging thousands of them to step out in faith and obedience on their campuses.

The meetings were held in the National Armory building in Washington and dozens of hotels were booked solid with rooms for these young people—often three and four in a room. One hotel manager said he was amazed that there was absolutely no damage in the rooms, only a few pillow cases ripped because of a fun-filled pillow fight!

As part of my role as president of YFC, I was occasionally privileged to spend a week or ten days in various parts of the country, often times with the local area director.

I recall one fall season being with my friend Bob Simpson in western Canada. We had eight or ten meetings night by night in small towns in Alberta and Saskatchewan. Oftentimes little country churches would be packed to the sides with young people. Various local talent would supply the music and I had the joy of preaching the message. Time after time I witnessed first-hand evidence of Jesus' Word that "the harvest is ripe."

On another occasion, for eight or nine days I traveled with the Palermo brothers, Phil and Louis, across eastern Pennsylvania. Night by night we had meetings in different churches in places like York, Harrrisburg, Lancaster and other towns where the Palermos were so very popular. (Incidentally, it was always a humorous experience to travel with those two. Each would take turns driving in their large van filled with instruments, books and material. While traveling, I would sit each day in the passenger's seat and whichever of the boys was not driving would give instructions to the driver from the back seat in a stream of consciousness monologue of wisecracks and creative banter. It was hilarious indeed.) The Lord blessed in these meetings again and again. Seemingly everywhere in the YFC programs in those day young people came to faith in Christ. The evangelical call to personal faith and dynamic daily obedience to God's Word, and a call to go and do likewise, was falling on receptive young hearts.

One of the highlights of my tenure in the leadership of Youth for Christ International was the establishing of Teen Teams who ministered across the world. I asked one of my special colleagues, Wendy Collins, to head up this program and he did a magnificent job year by year of bringing together teams of six, seven or eight talented young people, who became well trained in evangelism, to minister in many different areas of the world. The teams included musicians and an older youth leader who was generally the evangelist. They were booked in hundreds of meetings by the local YFC personnel.

In those years scores of Teen Teams ministered all across the globe—in numerous countries in Africa, all across Europe, in many places in Asia and throughout South America. Not only were those who were ministered to encouraged, blessed and many converted, but the challenge of ministry to these teenagers who formed the teams and their leadership training was tremendously significant. Most of the team members developed a vision for the world that influenced them to be world Christians for a lifetime.

During this period, on a visit to Germany with a couple of my YFC colleagues, we had the unusual pleasure of spending two or three hours one afternoon in the home of the famed Lutheran minister Martin Niemoller who served in Hitler's Germany. Niemoller continually preached against the Nazi persecution of Jews in concentration camps, even after being warned to stop and being threatened with arrest. Many times Nazi officials sat in his church to intimidate him by making notes. Finally they had had enough and Niemoller was arrested. The next morning, in jail, the chaplain, who was also a Lutheran minister, stopped by and expressed surprise at seeing his friend behind bars. The chaplain said, "Brother, what did you do? Why are you here?" Niemoller's facinating response was, "Brother, given what's happening in our country, why are you not in here?"

Other highlights of these years included several visits to Latin America—particularly a special visit to radio station HCJB, high in the Andes in Quito, Ecuador. Christian radio could reach hearts, especially in remote areas, as few ministries could. While there, I was the special guest of my beloved friend, Bob Savage, longtime missionary evangelist and radio personality in South America, the son of Dr. Henry Savage, pastor of the First Baptist Church in Pontiac, Michigan. Bob not only had me interviewed on that station whose broadcasts reached across much of South America, but also invited me to preach in the Christian and Missionary Alliance Church, established in the capital for English-speaking personnel. It was a great delight to share in fellowship with these godly missionary families who ministered through that pioneer missionary outlet, as well as with the expatriates assigned to that country.

Toward the end of this decade I was invited by the leadership of Youth for Christ in Australia and New Zealand to visit these burgeoning new programs. I invited one of our board members from Toledo, Ohio, a businessman named Sam Bender, to accompany me on this exhilarating though exhausting trip—literally traveling and ministering around the world. Sam's friendship, practical wisdom, and testimony were a great blessing as we shared in dozens of engagements together.

One night, in a large Youth for Christ rally in Auckland, New Zealand's capital, the most prominent auto race driver in the country publicly acknowledged his need for Christ by coming forward at the invitation and genuinely surrendered his life to the Savior. We had fellowship with him following the meeting with some of his new Christian friends.

During the trip Sam and I flew from Hong Kong to Saigon, and lifting off at the Hong Kong airport was one of the most frightening experiences of my life. Evidently some birds had gotten into the jets of the Convair airplane and we were barely able to lift off the rather short runway. The cabin attendant was so frightened that he could hardly make the announcement regarding our possible emergency landing into the sea. The plane struggled to gain altitude. Finally the captain was able to reassure us that the danger had passed and we were able to fly safely into Vietnam.

We traveled on for some engagements in South Vietnam and from there to the kingdom of Jordan, where we we the guests of His Royal Highness, King Hussein. This monarch was very kind to us and listened to us for forty-five minutes as we told him of the spiritual hunger of teens across the world and of the ministries focused on introducing them to new life in Christ. He hosted us for a time of tea together with some of his associates, in this rather unique contact point between two cultures and two diverse worldviews.

The vice president of Youth for Christ at that time, Roy McKeown, joined us in Jordan and accompanied us on to Israel, Vienna, and then on to Russia. We had no official contacts in

Russia at that time, but were able to find the one large Baptist church in the city where we went for Sunday morning worship. We arrived there early and an hour before the services began; the church was packed. Very kindly one of the ushers gave us a choice spot as visitors in the front row of the balcony.

Though we did not understand the Russian language as it was preached, we did sense the warmth of the people and their genuine desire to worship God. Following the service one of the several pastors in the church invited us in to the small pastor's study where we had a cup of coffee together and conversed as best we could with our lack of Russian and with his limited English but very warm heart. It was an occasion long to be remembered.

On another occasion, flying back from engagements in Manila to the States on Philippine Airlines, I was a special guest of the Christian president of the airline, John Sycip, who provided a sleeping bunk for me on one of his Clipper aircraft. It was the first and only time I was able to have a bed to sleep all the way home, with stops in Guam and Honolulu. I didn't even bother to get out of my bunk to go into the airport at those stops. I was too comfortable in my bunk—compliments of my friend!

My mentor during the early days of Youth for Christ was my very special friend, Bob Cook. I learned so very much from this godly man who had a permanent and unforgettable influence upon my life and walk with God.

For instance, at one time when I was facing some particular difficulty—long since forgotten—I said to Bob, "I'm through. I quit!" I know we've all been at that deeply frustrating point.

I will never forget Bob's response. "Fine, Ted, go ahead. But remember, it's always too soon to quit!" That's what I needed, and I hung in there.

When Bob resigned the presidency of Youth for Christ in 1957 to become vice president of Scripture Press, as indicated earlier, the board of YFC invited me to succeed. Obviously, this was a tremendous challenge, but a role in which I delighted in the Lord's guidance and direction, and in Bob's care-filled mentoring.

One of the joys of this particular period in my life was being associated with a host of godly colleagues in our Wheaton headquarters office. The quality and commitment of their lives created great synergy in YFC's expanding ministries. People like Hubert Mitchell, who was our first overseas director; Sam Wolgemuth, who followed Hubert in that role; Evon Hedley, executive director; "Kelly" Bihl, one of our first staff evangelists; Jack Hamilton, the International Bible Club director; Bill Eakin, Jack's associate in the Club program; Peter Quist, our business administrator; Louise Alfors, office manager; Jack Daniels, our regional director; Jay Kesler, youth evangelist and later to become YFC president and then president at Taylor University; Mel Larson, Warren Wiersbe, Harold Myra and Vern McLellan as editors of our YFC magazine; Bruce Love, the local chapter director; and a host of other wonderfully gifted young leaders across the nation.

Lorayne Edberg, who had previously been secretary to George Wilson, manager of the Billy Graham Evangelistic Association office in Minneapolis, was my faithful secretary for all of those years. In fact, when my family and I left Wheaton to come to California some years later she joined me as my secretary in my World Vision responsibilities.

My tenure of leadership with Youth for Christ International brought me into personal contact with some striking and interesting personalities outside of the organization too. For example, Dr. A.W. Tozer, one of the most gifted writers and preachers of that period, addressed our YFC leadership team in a special day-long seminar in Chicago. Dr. Tozer was a brilliant theologian and writer whose books have circulated by the hundreds of thousands over these years. In his address to the staff, Dr. Tozer decried the spiritual dryness among evangelicals and shared with us an impassioned plea for all of us to encounter God in all His majesty. It was the kind of absolutely unforgettable experience which God's Spirit used to permanently affect our own personal *Pursuit of God*, one of his great books.

Another fascinating personality, one who joined our YFC board during this period, was Herbert J. Taylor, president of the large Club Aluminum organization. Herb Taylor was a prominent Rotarian, serving as president of the largest Rotary Club in the world in Chicago. He was also the author of the famous Rotary Four Way Test: 1) Is it the truth? 2) Is it fair to all concerned? 3) Will it build good will and better friendship? 4) Will it be beneficial to all concerned? Mr. Taylor served on a score or more of evangelical boards and was tremendously influential in shaping the direction of much of the Christian community across the nation. (And for twenty-five years I was a member of the Arcadia Rotary Club.)

Taylor loved the Word of God deeply and had memorized Matthew 5-7, the Sermon on the Mount, which he repeated every morning. He was a tremendous influence on all of us younger men in the leadership of Youth for Christ, inspiring us to "follow hard after Christ."

Significant evangelistic youth crusades began to spring up all across the nation, as increasing numbers of youth were responding to public invitations to follow Christ. Evangelists who led these included such gifted preachers as Merv Rosell who had trained under Dr. W.B. Riley in Minneapolis; Jack Shuller, the son of Robert "Fighting Bob" Shuller, the Methodist radio preacher from Los Angeles; Charles Templeton, the eloquent youth leader from Toronto; Torrey Johnson, and Bob Cook.

Obviously, the move of my family from Grand Rapids to Wheaton, from book publishing to youth evangelism, was a major one—but was both exciting and eminently fulfilling. We purchased a home in Wheaton and for the first year or two I commuted by train to our YFC office at 220 N. Wells Street, on the Chicago Loop. After some months, Bob Cook and I decided to look for office property in Wheaton where we both had our homes. Subsequently, in 1954, we purchased a two-story building in the downtown business section of Wheaton, a former dry cleaning establishment. Later in the 1950's we built a much larger headquarters building on Gundersen Drive on the north side of the city. Our friend Stanley Kresge, of the large Kresge chain of stores (the corporate predecessor of K-mart), became a special benefactor and friend who helped us substantially in funding the new headquarters building.

One of the delights and benefits of our move to Wheaton was to be associated with a host of evangelical organizations who headquartered in this "Evangelical Vatican." Such close proximity enhanced trust and fellowship and brought great personal joy for me through the opportunity to interact with these significant ministries. God had truly done a special thing in Wheaton and intended the city to be of service to many in America and much of the world.

Included in those who headquartered in Wheaton were Scripture Press Publications, Van Kampen Press, The Evangelical Alliance Mission (TEAM), Pioneer Girls, The National Association of Evangelicals, Tyndale Publishers, Baptista Films, The Chapel of The Air, The Greater European Mission, The Sword of the Lord and Singspiration. And, of course, there was the strong, redemptive influence of the leadership at Wheaton College.

Sharing friendships, ideas, and needs with individuals from these various ministries was part of the delight of living in Wheaton. During this time, I made the acquaitnance of a special, rather unusual friend—the fundamentalist preacher, Dr. John R. Rice. He was a study: bombastic in the pulpit yet gentle as we met on the street. Dr. Rice and Mrs. Rice were avid golfers and I enjoyed several golf matches with them. What a sight they were on the course, with Mrs. Rice in a dress to her ankles and the doctor with his straw hat and long sleeved white shirt!

Dr. Rice was adamantly opposed to any involvement of women in ministry, even though he was the father of three daughters (no sons) and one wife. A classic piece of his thinking was seen in his book entitled *Bobbed Hair, Bossy Wives and Women Preachers*. In this book he argued that not only have the "modern, masculine, pants-wearing, cigarette smoking, bobbed hair women...fallen from her pedestal," but by taking to the pulpit she was violating "the command of God" against speaking "before mixed audiences." Dr. Rice was convinced that "this sin" was deeply hindering "the work of the Gospel of Christ." Yet, in person, he was mild and soft-spoken. Given a pulpit, he became a totally different individual. Though I disagreed with his view of women in ministry, he was a valued friend.

In 1957 Billy Graham conducted his significant New York City Crusade in Madison Square Garden. This was front page news. The Crusade lasted for 16 weeks with capacity crowds of 18,000 in the Garden every evening and audiences of 10 million-plus reached by the Saturday night telecasts across the nation. An estimated two million people heard Billy preach at the Garden, in Yankee Stadium, at Central Park, on Wall Street and in Brooklyn. During this period over 10,000 letters a day were received by the team with hundreds telling of decisions for Christ which swamped the Crusade office.

It was during these New York City meetings that Billy invited our Youth for Christ International board of directors to come to the Crusade as his guests, indicating that he would be pleased to meet with us for a period of the day when we had our board session there. We were deeply impressed by sharing in the Crusade services for a couple of nights and then to have Dr. Graham come in the midst of his tremendously stressful days to meet with us for several hours and to encourage all of us in the work of evangelism through Youth for Christ.

The missionary emphasis of YFC had no more able promoter than Bob Pierce, who had directed the YFC Rally in Seattle. Bob had led YFC preaching teams on tours throughout China and other parts of Asia in the late 40s and witnessed literally thousands who responded to the Gospel message during these campaigns. As Pierce went to Korea in 1950, he encountered the ravages of war in that nation. He was moved by the suffering of the people and came home and organized scores of World Vision rallies across the U.S. and Canada to enlist support. This was the beginning of World Vision, Inc. of which more will be written in our next chapter.

Early in the 1950s Dorothy and I purchased a small cottage at the Maranatha Bible Conference on the shores of Lake Michigan, near Muskegon, Michigan. It was a special bonus to have the family there during the summer season and be under the influence of some of the great Bible teachers who came to minister week by week. My special friend, Dr. Henry Savage, pastor of the First Baptist Church in Pontiac, Michigan, was the president of the Conference and a great friend. Howard Skinner was the director of the program throughout the summer. The Saturday night musicals, guided by Howard and Ada Skinner, added so much to the joy and worship of these events, season by season.

During this period of time Youth for Christ sponsored a leadership training program at the Conference grounds, led by my colleague Kelly Bihl. Literally hundreds of youth leaders were trained in these week-long sessions in this attractive and appealing environment. Over the years an army of lay leaders' skills were sharpened through such events for greater service as laborers in the spiritual harvest.

On one of my visits to the Orient, Dick Hillis, founder of Overseas Crusades, then headquartering in Taiwan, asked me to go with him to the Japanese island of Okinawa to share in a ministry among the American troops who were there. We spent two days together in Naha, the capital, in what was a very difficult missions challenge. Being with this outstanding missionary leader, who had been evacuated from China with other missionaries some years previous, was a memorable experience. Later on that trip I had the privilege of spending a night or two with the Hillises in Taipei.

Dick had a twin brother, Don, who was a missionary in India. Following service in India with the Evangelical Alliance Mission, he and his family lived in Wheaton for a period of time, where we formed a warm friendship. The Hillis twins made a remarkable impact in those years upon the cause of Christ in their leadership responsibilities.

Following our move to Wheaton, Dorothy and I were invited to share in some consultations with a few friends on the possibility of forming a new congregation related to the Evangelical Free Church. Among those interested in this new church were Carl Gundersen, a successful contractor and chairman of the board of the Evangelical Alliance Mission; Bob Van Kampen, Christian publisher; Paul Johnson, a sales manager; and Charles Hennix, an executive of the Elgin Watch Company—along with our wives. We met on several occasions in the basement of the large Gundersen home, where the first several meetings of the new congregation were also held. Later we rented the Masonic Hall in the city for our Sunday morning worship.

Wendell Loveless, popular Christian personality on Moody Bible Institute's radio station WMBI and well-known gospel song writer, was invited to be our first pastor. He had a significant ministry with this exciting new fellowship. The congregation grew by leaps and bounds and after a year or so we decided to build a church on the main east-west highway, Roosevelt Road, going through Wheaton. The church was built in the mid 1950s and was called The Church by the Side of the Road. It became a strong witness in the Evangelical Free Church denomination and has since become one of the prime churches in the entire EV Church fellowship.

It was during this time that I received an invitation from the Ministry of Tourism in Israel to bring a group of youth leaders to that nation to be exposed to its Old Testament history. Teddy Kollack, then director of the Tourism Bureau and later to be the popular mayor of Jerusalem, personally invited me to come to Jerusalem to discuss this possibility. He supplied me with my El Al airline ticket and hosted me at the King David Hotel.

The hoped-for youth leader meeting did not materialize but it was a fascinating experience to be the guest of the Israeli government to explore the possibilities of such an arrangement for Christian leaders to visit that Jewish nation.

Dwight Eisenhower was president during this decade and was a popular national figure. On one occasion, prior to our YFC Capital Teen convention, Roy McKeown, director of the convention, and I were invited to sit on the platform the afternoon that the President lit the famous White House Christmas tree. One of our YFC groups from Santa Barbara, led by the director Fred Sanborn, supplied the Christmas music for that occasion. The president very graciously thanked both Roy and me for our participation in the program.

On another occasion, I was privileged to attend a press conference which President Eisenhower conducted. It was interesting to be with the large group of reporters from the media—radio, print and television—who participated in the interrogating of the President.

Sixteen and thirty-five millimeter Gospel films became increasingly popular during this decade. The Moody Science films showed the wonder of God's creation in explaining numerous scientific discoveries. The Great Commission films produced a number of popular films used in churches. Bob Pierce developed most of his World Vision films during the 1950s, including the award-winning *Cry in the Night*, the excellent *38th Parallel* about Korea and *China Challenge* concerning ministries in China just prior to the collapse of that government to the Communists.

It was during the days of the Korean conflict in the early part of the decade that Bob Pierce called me one day and asked if I could possibly supply him with an accreditation card indicating that he was a war correspondent. I was editing the *Christian Digest* at Zondervan at the time and unofficially appointed him our war correspondent! I had a small wallet-size card printed indicating that "Dr. Bob Pierce was an official correspondent for the *Christian Digest!*" He was able to flash that card wherever he went, opening doors for him that only correspondents were able to walk through!

Near the close of the 1950s I received a call one day from Billy Graham asking me if I could spend a day with him at his mother's home in Charlotte, North Carolina. It's interesting to recall that Billy met me at the airport and we drove down the highway which later was to be named the Billy Graham Freeway.

His reason for asking me to come to Charlotte was to explore with me the possibility of my editing a magazine he had in mind which later became *Decision* magazine. It was a fascinating time talking about the vision that he had for the publication, but I didn't feel at that time that this was what the Lord would have for me. Obviously, over the years this publication has had a tremendous influence upon millions of people across the world, being translated in a number of languages.

Early in the 1950s Bill Jones, a Christian businessman who had a large printing business in Los Angeles, had a burden for bringing our national leadership together for a prayer breakfast in the nation's capital. It was during the time of the Eisenhower presidency that Bill invited several hundred key leaders from across the country to meet with the president, members of Congress, members of the Supreme Court and national leadership in what was then know as the Presidential Prayer Breakfast. Jones footed the bill for this breakfast, which since has become the annual international Prayer Breakfast, with 3,000 and more in attendance. Later hotel man Conrad Hilton picked up the tab for the breakfast over a period of several years.

I had the privilege of attending this first Prayer Breakfast with President Eisenhower as a special guest of my friend Bill Jones, as well as numerous subsequent national Prayer Breakfasts. Each one has proved to be a moving event, reminding our leadership of the vital importance of humbling ourselves and asking God to be at the center of leadership of our national life.

During this decade I was very much involved in activities at my alma mater, Taylor University. In the early 50sI served as president of the Alumni Association and then later was invited to join the board of trustees. My friend Dr. Evan Bergwall was the president of the university at the time and it was a delight to work closely with him for a period as chairman of the board. The college made great strides during Bergwall's leadership with a significant increase in the student body population year by year and full accreditation from the North Central Association of Colleges and Universities.

These responsibilities called for frequent visits to the campus and interacction with many of the students who have since gone on to significant service for the Lord across the world.It was during this time as well that the university honored me with a doctorate—doctor of humane letters.

A key player in the revival movement of the 1950s was my very special friend Armin Gesswein. Armin was a minister in the Lutheran Church—Missouri Synod who had experienced a marvelous conversion under the preaching of evangelist Paul Rader. Armin felt called to the ministry and went to study at Concordia Theological Seminary in St. Louis, where the well-known radio preacher Walter Maier was a professor. During his first pastorate, Gesswein began to have fellowship with evangelicals who were outside the Lutheran fold. Evidently, this practice got him in trouble with the strictly separatist Missouri Synod.

Dismayed by his denomination's sectarian spirit, at that time, Gesswein resigned his pastorate and became the minister of an independent church. Earlier on, while conducting a preaching tour in Norway, he encountered a revival that was sweeping through both the state-sponsored Lutheran and the Free churches. He came home inspired about what he had witnessed and determined to see a revival of that kind happen in the United States. (Before he left Norway, he met his future wife, Reidun.)

Armin began to travel from city to city on a teaching mission, holding retreats and establishing prayer meetings for revival among pastors of many denominations. He was a great promoter of revival and prayer within the YFC movement.

Another key figure in the evangelical world during this period of the 50s was Henrietta Mears, director of religious education at the Hollywood Presbyterian Church. Miss Mears ("Teacher") inspired and challenged hundreds of Southern California's young adults. She was a wealthy, talented and vibrant woman who had worked for several years at the First Baptist Church in Minneapolis and later came to the Hollywood Church. In three years she built the Sunday school enrollment from 450 pupils to more than 5,000. Faced with the lack of evangelical curriculum materials for Sunday schools, Miss Mears created her own and founded Gospel Light Publications to market them.

Ministry to young adults was her passion, and she took special delight in challenging them to engage in their own ministries. One of her proteges was Bill Bright, who began a program among UCLA students. Bright urged Miss Mears to provide a place for college age young adults to hold retreats, so she developed Forest Home, a beautiful, large conference center in the San Bernardino mountains. Over 600 students attended the first college briefing she conducted.

Miss Mears also opened her home in Westwood for people in show business, attracting such stars as Roy Rogers and Dale Evans. And, with the help of revivalist Edwin Orr, her weekly gathering soon was attracting up to 40 Hollywood entertainers and movie people.

One night late in the decade, Dick Hillis, the missionary to Taiwan (then called Formosa), called me about midnight to indicate a vision he had for an athletic missionary team to come to Formosa to play exhibition basketball games and to share a Christian witness. He wondered if I knew someone who could head up such a project. I indicated to him that my friend, Don Odle, basketball coach at Taylor University, was an outstanding committed Christian and a superb coach. I assured him that I would be glad to talk to Don to see what interest he might have in such a project.

The next day I did so and Coach Odle responded immediately to the challenge. The end result of all of this was that the coach formed a basketball squad of young athletes from various Christian colleges who went to the Orient the following summer, both to play basketball and primarily to bring a witness for Christ. This was called Venture for Victory which continued on year by year for a decade beyond that initial contact with Dick Hillis. In following years they ministered in Korea, Hong Kong and the Philippines. In addition, as a result of his contacts, Coach Odle was asked to coach the Chinese (Formosa) basketball team at the 1960 Olympics held in Rome.

The 1950s closed for me in a most dramatic—and miraculous—fashion. Youth for Christ was sponsoring a large Congress on Evangelism to be held the first days of 1960 in Madras, India. Several thousand teenagers and their adult counselors were scheduled to be in Madras, both from across all of India and other parts of Asia. I was to lead a team of forty American adult leaders to share in this Congress. We were to leave the day after Christmas, December 26, from New York city, fly to Israel to spend a few days, then move on to Lebanon for a day, arriving in India on January 2 to begin the leadership of the Congress.

On Christmas Eve, I received a late evening phone call from my colleague in Washington, Sam Wolgemuth, who had been working with the Indian Embassy there with last minute details related to our American passports and visas. Almost panic-stricken, Sam indicated to me that the Indian government in New Delhi had ordered the cancellation of all the visas in our passports.

I was so stunned I scarcely knew which way to turn. I asked the Lord for guidance from His Word that night, and a verse from the First epistle of John popped off the page of my Bible in which the Apostle had written, "God is greater!" I said to the Lord late that Christmas Eve this situation that was a wonderful opportunity to prove that He was greater than governments or the influences of man!

I went to New York to meet my colleagues on December 26 and told them of the challenge facing us, and indicated that we would refund their travel costs if they did not desire to move forward. However, I said to them that I felt like Moses facing the Red Sea and was willing to press on to see how the Lord might work. They all responded, "Let's go!"

We left Sam Wolgemuth back in Washington to wrestle with the problem and moved on to the Holy Land.

On December 31 we had a very wonderful and moving service in Jerusalem at Gordon's Garden tomb. T.W. Wilson, of the Billy Graham Association, led us in our devotional time and prayer in front of this simple but beautiful tomb in the heart of Jerusalem. With us was Mr. Solomon Mattar, a wonderful Arab Christian and the keeper of the tomb. He and his family lived in that lovely Garden area.

While we were at the Garden tomb for the service, Mr. Mattar invited two or three of us to walk with him into the empty tomb. It had a very low and narrow entrance, but we squeezed in one at a time into the tomb. While inside we had a time of prayer together thanking God for the risen Savior.

As we were about to close the service, a messenger came from the hotel nearby where we had been staying, indicating that there was a long distance phone call awaiting me. I raced back to get the phone call and learned that it was from Sam in Washington.

He said, "Ted, you and the group go to Beirut, as planned, tomorrow and report at 4 P.M. to the Indian Embassy there. They will have the passports stamped for you."

"Sam," I said, "no embassy in the world is open on New Year's Day! And, as you know, once a visa has been cancelled out of a passport new passports must be reissued."

Sam said, "Do as I say. Report tomorrow afternoon in Beirut."

We did. And, much to our amazement and with deep gratitude, the embassy was opened for all forty of us on this New Year's Day. They did indeed re-stamp our passports with an Indian visa, an unprecedented event.

We arrived in Madras right on schedule, ready to begin that wonderful series of events in the large pandal (tent) which the folks there had erected on the grounds of the Emmanuel Methodist Church. It was a magnificent event and scores of choice Indian young people were challenged to service as a result of the congress sessions.

A year later, I was back in Jerusalem and was a guest for lunch at the home of the Mattars. During our conversation I asked, "Brother Mattar, do you remember our being here a year ago and our time together in the tomb? It was an unforgettable experience for me." I knew that he had conducted scores of tours of Christian pilgrims over the years to that spot. Probably our tour group was nothing special.

However, Mr. Mattar said, "You know, brother Ted, that was a most unusual experience for me. Something happened that day that had never happened before—or since. While we were standing there I heard a voice say to me—not audibly but in my heart—'Son, you have represented me well here today.' I had never experienced that before, but on the day that your friends were there the Lord spoke to me in approval of my message to you all regarding the glorious resurrection of our Lord Jesus Christ."

It was not long after that second visit that my friend, Mr. Mattar, was cruelly murdered by Israeli troops on the grounds of his beloved Garden tomb.

"A key event marking the spiritual rebellion of the time was the 1962 Supreme Court decision which banned prayer and Bible reading in public schools. This ruling reflected the growing feeling that God had no place formally in our lives and society anymore, which signaled the beginning of the most sweeping moral demise in the history of our nation."

3

REFLECTIONS

The 1960s – The Decade of Rebellion

THE LEGACIES OF THE 60s INCLUDED A LEGACY OF A godless society and a spiritual vacuum in our nation still felt to this day. The moral free–fall of earlier decades accelerated during these years.

A brighter side of the 60s rebellion, symbolized in December of 1963, was the famous Dr. Martin Luther King, Jr's speech during the March on Washington at the Lincoln Memorial. In that speech, which brought him to the pinnacle of his fame, he declared, "I have a dream" for racial equality and reconciliation. It was a positive rebellion against the social injustice of the decade. Great passion was released for those who suffered from racial prejudice. Many expressed compassion as well as anger against the Vietnam war, indicating that there was a better way than napalm and bombs in solving conflict. An accompanying legacy of the decade was that social justice demands social action.

A Nobel Peace Prize came to King in 1964, and that same year Congress passed the Civil Rights Act, followed by the Voting Rights Act in 1965.

Upon reflection, the decade of the 60s was said by many to be The Decade of Rebellion. It was marked, for example, by such events as the sixty hours at Woodstock, New York, where 40,000 young people gathered to declare that rebellion had triumphed, raising immorality to a new level. It was marked by a severe anti-authority, "in your face" spirit symbolized by the song "Born to be Wild."

A key event marking the spiritual rebellion of the time was the 1962 Supreme Court decision which banned prayer and Bible reading in public schools. This ruling reflected the growing feeling that God had no place formally in our lives and society anymore, which signaled the beginning of the most sweeping moral demise in the history of our nation. A moral and spiritual dam seemed to break, similar to the Old Testament image of a "stiff necked peo-ple" and proving the proverb that "pride goes before a fall."

In addition there were enormously significant international events which marked the decade. It was during this period of time that the East German leadership built the infamous Berlin Wall to stop a large-scale exodus of citizens from the East. It was in the midst of the decade that the Arab-Israeli war and the U.S. military support of Israel brought much of the Arab world into the Soviet orbit.

Nationally, early in the decade The Bay of Pigs invasion of Cuba took place, John Glenn became the first American to orbit the earth and James Meredith was the first black student to attend the University of Mississippi.

In 1963 the inspirational President John F. Kennedy was assassinated. During the middle of the decade came the destruc-tive Los Angeles Watts riots—and later in the decade, both Martin Luther King, Jr. and Robert Kennedy were assassinated. Indeed it was the "Decade of Rebellion!"

———————

Following the years of leadership given to Youth for Christ during the 50s, I felt in my heart that it was time to make a change in my career path. I sensed that I had given all that I could to that ministry and it should now have new and different leadership. Thus, in January of 1963, I announced my resignation to the YFC Board, effective in the spring.

Meanwhile, shortly after announcing the resignation, I was in Washington D.C., to attend the annual Presidential Prayer Breakfast. On an aside, it has been my privilege to meet with three U.S. presidents—President Nixon (on a visit to the Seattle World's Fair when he was Vice President), President Jimmy Carter on several occasions, including a time in the White House Cabinet Room, and President Dwight Eisenhower. As I arrived at the Mayflower Hotel I was met in the lobby by Dr. Bob Pierce, founder and president of World Vision. As indicated earlier, Bob and I first met in 1946. Over the intervening years, he had visited our home in both Michigan and Illinois on numerous occasions and I had been with him often on business trips to Southern California. Several times I was interviewed by Bob on his Mutual Network Sunday afternoon radio broadcast for World Vision.

As we greeted in the hotel lobby, Bob asked if we might have coffee together in the coffee shop. I checked into my room and shortly thereafter I met him for the time of fellowship. Bob indicated that he had been in Chicago the previous two days fasting and praying concerning his World Vision program. He had lost his executive vice president and quite evidently the ministry needed an operating executive. Bob said, "Ted, as I have been praying and fasting these last days, the Lord laid your name on my heart. Would you consider leaving Youth for Christ and coming with me as our executive officer?"

"Bob." I said, "It will surprise you to know that I have just tendered my resignation to YFC."

Bob began to weep and said, "The Lord has answered my prayers. You are going to come with me."

I responded that I was looking at several other opportunities and wasn't at all sure that this was what the Lord had in mind for me. However, Bob asked that I come to California to meet with his board and explore the possibility, which I agreed to do.

Some weeks later I did meet with the World Vision board in Pasadena. Present were several prominent leaders, some of whom I knew and others I would come to know very well, including Dr. Dick Halverson, one of the pastors at the Hollywood Presbyterian Church, later pastor of the significant Fourth Presbyterian Church in Washington, D.C. and then Chaplain of the United States Senate until his death in 1996; Cliff Barrows, of the Billy Graham Evangelistic Association; Senator Frank Carlson of Kansas; Dr. Carlton Booth, professor of evangelism at Fuller Seminary; and Claude Edwards, chairman of the board of a large grocery marketing firm in Southern California.

The board, with Bob Pierce, offered me the position of executive vice president. I promised to counsel with Dorothy about it, pray and give them a response in a few weeks. The Lord did indeed give guidance and in the summer of 1963 our family moved to Arcadia, California, and I began my long tenure with this international evangelistic and relief agency.

My last official set of duties with Youth for Christ International, prior to my coming with World Vision in 1963, was to have a three-week evangelistic visit to South Africa, under the sponsorship of SAYFC. It was my privilege to share in youth rallies in practically all of the major cities of South Africa during that period of time including Cape Town, Johannesburg, Durban, Bloemfontein, Port Elizabeth, and Pretoria. In addition, I was the guest speaker for the first YFC camp held in a lovely place called Carmel. Over 200 teenagers came together for the week. It was a delightful experience to share with those young people, concerns of discipleship and their commitment to follow Jesus in the years ahead.

It's interesting to note that in years following, on subsequent visits to that nation, invariably people would come to me in meetings to tell me that it was through those series of YFC rallies across the nation that they came to faith in Christ. What an encouragement that has been to my heart.

Many choice friendships were formed during those days, including that with my friend Dr. Louw Alberts, a confidant of political leaders and one of the strongest voices for evangelicalism in South Africa. Louw is an internationally recognized physicist, popular public speaker and a person of great influence. I also shared in the meetings with Jimmy Ferguson, the YFC director in the nation, Denis Clark, a prominent evangelist and Dennis House, who later became the director of YFC, South Africa. As a result of these and other visits, South Africa has become one of my favorite nations among the countries that I have visited over the six decades of my experience.

——— ——— ———

If the editors of *Reader's Digest* were to ask me to write a chapter for their popular feature, "My Most Unforgettable Character," I would immediately think of Bob Pierce. He was without a doubt the most complex, fascinating individual I had ever known or met. In many ways he was a classic schizophrenic.

No man I've ever known had a greater compassion for suffering, hurting people—particularly children—in the world. He loved people intensely and his heart continually went out to those who were displaced, disenfranchised, suffering and hurting. One of his great joys was entertaining missionaries as he traveled, hosting delightful dinner occasions for them in the finest hotels in their cities.

Bob was tremendously generous, constantly aiding national leaders and Christian workers with a purchase of a refrigerator, a jeep, paying back rentals or whatever was needed. He was both an evangelist and a Christian humanitarian. He saw clearly in Scripture the vital importance of bringing together the meeting of human need, the offering of the "cup of cold water" in Jesus' name, along with the proclamation of the Gospel. He loved to preach Gospel messages and was immensely effective in the many large evangelistic crusades he held in major cities across Asia as well as in literally hundreds of churches in America. Again, no one could burden people more or better than Bob in taking offerings in churches. He was a master offering-taker!

It is not my purpose to speak of the downside of my friend Bob, except to say that he often exploded with an uncontrollable temper and would repeatedly repent of his use of improper language. Oftentimes I would watch as he would prostrate himself before the Lord and repent of his intemperance in many parts of his character. He knew where the source of His compassion and generosity came from, and turned to the Lord innumerable times for fresh grace and strength.

It was a great learning experience for me to travel with Bob during my first years in World Vision.

The original World Vision offices, opened in early 1950, were in a building owned by the Navigators, with Dawson Trotman as director, in Eagle Rock, California. Later the offices were moved to two floors in an office building in downtown Pasadena, where I first had my office. In 1964 we built a large 35,000 square foot headquarters in Monrovia, on some property which had been purchased earlier through our stewardship department. This property included several acres on which additional buildings were erected in the years following. It served as headquarters for all of the World Vision ministries reaching out across the globe.

Early on in my new role with Bob Pierce, he asked me to accompany him on a trip to Japan and Korea. Bob often referred to Korea as his "second home." He loved it and the people very deeply and they in turn highly respected and appreciated him as their close friend. The Korean war in the early 50s, the terrible physical needs of orphans and lepers, and the spiritual vitality of the people bound Bob to Korea in a permanent and unique manner.

On this first visit I was introduced to scores of "orphan superintendents" who headed up our various World Vision orphanages scattered across the Korean peninsula. I was also introduced to the beautiful Children's Hospital in Seoul which Dr. Pierce had designed and for which he raised all of the funds. It certainly was a center of mercy for crippled, undernourished, sick children who were brought in from all across the country. This visit also included time spent in the World Vision sponsored schools for the blind and the deaf.

The director of our program in Korea at the time was Reverend Irv Raetz and his gifted wife, Florence. "Uncle Irv" had significant experience previously in Asia as director of the

Christian's Children's Fund. Working closely with him as associate director were my dear friends Marlin and Kay Nelson, who later succeeded the Raetzes as directors of the program in Korea. They served in this role significantly for more than twenty years, prior to Marlin's becoming a faculty member of the newly formed Asia Center for Theological Studies (ACTS). World Vision supplied the funding for this new seminary and has supported since. I was asked to serve as a member of the Board of Directors of ACTS in the U.S., a role I have had the pleasure of sharing to this day.

No country has made a greater impression upon me than Korea and its lovely people. Over the years I have visited there as many as a dozen or more times, and each time I am impressed with the vitality of these people who have bounced back from the trauma of the war in the early 1950s and which today have one of Asia's strongest economies. I have had the privilege of preaching in number of Korean churches and, in addition, have visited the Full Gospel Church in Seoul, which is the largest congregation in the world with over 600,000 members. Services are held at the church all day on Sunday, and every night of the week. Literally hundreds of small group Bible studies are held in homes across the city every evening, and hundreds share as well in around-the-clock prayer sessions on what is called a "prayer mountain" outside of the city, owned by the church, pastored by Paul Yongi Cho. I believe the Korean church has much to teach the body of Christ, especially in the West, about seeking the Lord in prayer—long and often.

One evening, while on a ministry tour in Japan with Bob Pierce, I was rooming with him in a Tokyo hotel. About 4 A.M. I was awakened by hearing Bob pray, in his sleep, loudly and earnestly, for the people in Japan to whom he had been ministering. I was greatly moved by this experience of a man who prayed so earnestly in his sleep. In the morning I asked Bob if he knew he had been praying while sleeping.

"No, buddy," he said, "But I know that God hears my prayers even in my dreams and sleep!"

This was typical of the burden and concern Bob Pierce had for the people for whom he was called to minister. Prayer was at the very heart of his life—even while asleep!

On another of my visits to Japan I was scheduled for some conferences in the ancient city of Kobe. I arrived rather late in the evening with my confirmed reservation for a nice hotel in the city but was told upon my arrival that there were no rooms available. I protested that I had a confirmed reservation, showed it to the clerk, but again was told that they had "no room in the inn."

I indicated that I would take a display room or any other accommodations that might be opened up for me. "No way," I was told.

Finally I said, "There must be someplace where I can sleep." The clerk said, "All we have is the Emperor's Suite." I responded, "I'll take it!" The astounded clerk then gave me the keys to this absolutely elegant suite of rooms—at the single room rate. It was the most elaborate hotel suite of rooms I have ever seen anywhere in the world! And, I slept like a baby.

With my responsibilities at World Vision, I wrote a monthly column for our *World Vision* magazine. In checking back, I note what I said in my first column, shortly after my arrival at the WV headquarters: "Although I have visited over fifty mission fields, this is my first trip as part of World Vision. "One haunting impression: it is impossible for us who live in North America to grasp the anguish, horrors and emptiness of stomachs and hearts of millions in bleak areas of the Orient. Two hundred million Indians, for example, live on less than $3 a month. Their diet is rice and pepper water once a day—sometimes one meal every other day.

God has called World Vision to move into the midst of such crying needs. Dr. Bob Pierce has long sensed the vital part medical work plays in meeting these situations head on. Thus World Vision has had a continuing program of aiding the medical care of children, lepers, the elderly and indigent.

In country after country, we visited World Vision supported medical centers—none pretentious—but all ministering faithfully in Christ's name. They included a skin clinic in Seoul, Korea, treating lepers and at the same time, constantly studying methods of curtailing leprosy in the children's wing of the great

Presbyterian Hospital in Taegu, Korea; the children's hospitals in Pingtung and Puli, Taiwan; and elsewhere.

In each of these, not only is splendid medical care offered, but love and compassion are extended in Christ's name, and desperately needy people are pointed to the One who said, "Come unto me."

World Vision has continually worked and ministered with various evangelical mission groups across the world. One of these close partners was the Norwegian Missionary Alliance with headquarters in Oslo, led by its general secretary, the Reverend Paul Walstad. Personnel from this group headed up much of the medical work supported by World Vision in both Korea and Taiwan. I found these Norwegian doctors and nurses to be among God's choicest servants on the mission field.

On several occasions I visited the hospital run by the Norwegian colleagues in Puli, Taiwan, among the Taiwanese nationals. This vibrant, effective ministry was led by Norwegian deacon Bjarre Gislefoss and his doctor wife, Dr. Ahlfild Gislefoss. In the heart of Taiwan hundreds of tubercular patients were treated monthly and an average of over 250 patients per month professed faith in the Lord Jesus Christ. Meeting both physical and spiritual needs was being accomplished by people who saw this same pattern in Jesus' ministry.

Similarly in the World Vision Children's Hospital in Pingtung, Taiwan, staffed by Dr. Kristopher Fotland and other Norwegian doctors and nurses, children received compassionate care and Christ was presented to each patient. These Norwegian workers became choice friends over the years and on one occasion I had the opportunity of visiting with them in their homeland of Norway for a special reunion of the workers ministering with us in Taiwan.

———

During my various travels with Dr. Pierce in the early days of my tenure with World Vision, it was a wonderful privilege to meet some key international leadership personalities. On one occasion, in Formosa (now Taiwan), we were invited to attend the morning worship service in the private chapel of

Generalissimo and Madame Chiang-Kai-shek in Taipei. Bob had earlier formed a friendship with the Generalissimo and his charming wife, and we were warmly greeted as we attended the service. The message, preached by the chaplain, was in Chinese but we readily recognized the warmth of the service, the Bible teaching and the sincere faith of the president of Formosa and much of his staff who were in attendance.

On the same Asia trip with Bob, while in New Delhi, the capital of India, we were invited to have a forty–five minute session with Madam Gandhi, the prime minister, in her private garden. There were only Bob and I, plus the prime minister and two of her aides, who spent the time together in which Bob shared his faith with her and told her of the work of World Vision in her country. The prime minister was a very charming individual, most gracious, who listened carefully to what we had to say. She wished us well in her country and complimented World Vision on its activities on behalf of many of the suffering people in that nation.

—————

During this decade the popular, well-received World Vision Korean Children's Choir made several tours of the United States and Canada—plus giving concerts throughout Asia. This group of youngsters, ages eight to fifteen, were wonderful representatives of World Vision and in their concerts enlisted hundreds of childcare sponsors for our organization.

Early on, during a visit to Korea at the World Vision Music School, I was attracted to a lovely little eight–year–old by the name of Hyung Ja Moon. I came home and told my family about this little "Dresden doll." On subsequent tours we "adopted" Hyung Ja into our family and she became a little "sister" to our JoAnn. On frequent visits to Korea I would always make contact with this young lady, take her to lunch and encourage her in her walk with the Lord.

Hyung Ja has a lovely contralto voice and was a soloist with the Children's Choir. After she graduated from the choir she became a part of a young ladies trio known as the Joy Bells who also subsequently toured throughout Korea, Japan and on a special ministry trip to the U.S.

Hyung Ja is now married to a pastor, served with him for two or three years among Koreans in Brazil, and is the mother of two lovely children. This is one of the truly happy success stories of sponsored children moving on to be responsible followers and servants of Christ.

———————

During the early part of my tenure at World Vision, I attended a school for executives exposed to the exploding computer world sponsored by the IBM corporation in San Jose, California. World Vision had just purchased a large IBM computer (a 1401) and I was completely ignorant concerning what it could do for us. I attended the school for a week, which opened my eyes to the amazing capabilities of our computerized society.

Upon returning home, the following Sunday morning I taught an adult Bible class at my home church, Lake Avenue Congregational Church in Pasadena. I tried to explain, rather awkwardly, how I felt that computers could be used to enhance the proclamation of the Gospel across the world. I know that I did not explain it very well, but I did have the burden to see this technology used in world evangelism.

A member of the class at that time, Ed Dayton, had just left a successful engineering career in Michigan to be enrolled at Fuller Theological Seminary. Following the class period he asked if we might have a lunch together, which we did. Ed, very knowledgeable in the arena of computers, said that he tracked with me in my concern—even though I was recognizably ignorant concerning what I was saying. That luncheon began a warm friendship and some months later I invited Ed to join our World Vision staff, following his graduation from Fuller, to head up an unknown arena which would strategize concerning how a computer world could be used by the Spirit of God to enhance the proclamation of the Gospel. Ed accepted the invitation and founded what became known as the Missions Advanced Research and Communications Center within World Vision. This MARC program, over the years, has made a tremendous impact upon missions, particularly in the area of reaching the unreached peoples of the world.

Not long after my arrival at World Vision, I arranged for the staff to begin meeting on a weekly basis for an hour's chapel service each Wednesday morning. When in the country, Bob Pierce would meet and share with us and we had a stream of key people who came to visit us and minister during that time. One of the highlights of the services was the visit on one occasion of the famed Dr. E. Stanley Jones, the eminent missionary states-man to India and the author of hosts of widely distributed books including *The Christ of the Indian Road*. It was a joy and delight to have Dr. Jones share with us in chapel and in fellowship throughout the day. Other chapel speakers during that period included such people as Dr. Carl F.H. Henry, Dr. Harold Lindsell, Dr. David Hubbard, Reverend Waiter Corlett of the Carey Memorial Church in Calcutta, Dr. John Stott, of London and hosts of others of international note.

One of the highlights for me in the 1960s was sharing in a pastors' conference in Nagaland, in northeast India. It was at the turn of the century that British missionaries came to the Naga Hills, populated by tribal people, and tens of thousands of these people were converted, forming churches all across that primi-tive, mountainous area of India. World Vision, under the guid-ance and direction of Dr. Paul Pees, was invited by the church in Nagaland to conduct a pastors' conference there in the little town of Mokokchung. Members of the team ministering at the confer-ence included Dr. Pees, Bob Pierce, Dick Halverson and myself.

It was very difficult for foreigners to enter Nagaland and it wasn't until the last half day before leaving Calcutta that we were able to secure the necessary permit to travel, first by air and then ten hours by jeep, to the Naga Hills. Much to our amaze-ment, more than 9,000 Christians awaited us at the site of the congress—when we were expecting only a few hundred. More than a pastors' conference, it was a wonderful gathering for six days of utterly delightful Christian believers. Our team stayed in a simple government "long house" and we were taken care of by a fine Indian Christian cook who supplied us with western meals!

All of the messages were translated into three or four of the tribal languages as the groups met in separate areas of a great pandal that had been erected for the occasion. It was an utterly remarkable occasion as the Spirit of God came upon that assembly, unlike anything I had ever previously experienced or witnessed. Warm friendships were formed and as a result, a Bible school was begun, which remains effectively active to this day.

In addition to Bob Pierce, three of my other colleagues in World Vision made a strong and enduring impact upon my life. All three were choice servants of God and among the most remarkable men I have ever known.

The first of these is my beloved friend Dr. Paul Pees. I first met Paul when I was a student at Taylor University. He came as a young minister to conduct a series of chapel services at the college. I served as his student aide during those days. Later Dr. Pees pastored the large First Covenant Church in Minneapolis, and in the late 1950s joined World Vision to direct the pastors' conferences, which were held in scores of places across the globe. Paul was internationally known as a "preacher to preachers" and was in great demand as a speaker, not only in North America but in many parts of the world. He was a gentle Christian, loving, open and a special spiritual mentor to me. I admired him as I did few men in my acquaintance.

A second remarkable man in my life was Dr. F. Carlton Booth. Carlton had a remarkable Christian career, serving early on as professor of music and evangelism at Providence Bible Institute (now Barrington College), as song evangelist in the Jack Wyrtzen Times Square *Word of Life* national radio broadcasts, and then professor of evangelism at Fuller Theological Seminary. Carlton was one of the earliest members of the World Vision board of directors and had a second office at the World Vision headquarters. He became to me my "Barnabas, Son of Encouragement." He was a special counselor to me in my World Vision leadership until his passing in the mid-1990s. He would share my confidences, pray for me and offer wise and sage counsel. He and his wife Ruth became very special friends to Dorothy and me over the decades. To this day I miss him, his wisdom and his friendship.

A third remarkable individual who was introduced in my life in this decade was Dr. Dick Halverson. Dick was a Presbyterian pastor, serving on the staff of the First Presbyterian Church of Hollywood, then for many years as pastor of the prestigious Fourth Presbyterian Church in the nation's capital. Later, until his death in 1994, he was chaplain of the U.S. Senate. For more than two decades Dick served as chairman of our World Vision board of directors, beginning in the earliest days when he was invited to be on the board by Bob Pierce. Dick had a passion for personal evangelism and for the role of the Church in the life of believers.

Again, he was a very special counselor to me and a very warm and generous supporter of my leadership in World Vision. During the period of Dr. Pierce's years of sabbatical leave, Dick served as our interim president from Washington, and we were in almost daily telephone contact. What a giant Dick was and what a very special friend to me.

All three of these great men are now with the Lord, and I can only think of them with the warmest of remembrances and with the deepest appreciation for what they meant in my life.

Three wonderful, godly women as well made an indelible impression upon me during this period of my ministry and travels.

The first of these is Mrs. Gladys Donnithorne. Mrs. Donnithorne, ("Aunt Gladys"), the wife of an Anglican archdeacon, spent most of her lifetime among the displaced, impoverished people in what was known as the Forbidden City in Hong Kong. Mrs. Donnithorne was a titled English lady who was not afraid of getting her hands dirty as she ministered to opium addicts, orphaned children and disenfranchised Chinese in the heart of the city, which in the 60s was recovering from the difficult days of war. She was supported by World Vision and every time I was with her, as she shared her burden and concern, I was deeply moved in my spirit to recognize the sacrifice of this dear lady as she ministered in Christ's name.

The second remarkable woman was Mrs. Lillian Dickson. Her husband was Dr. James Dickson, the head of the Presbyterian Seminary in Taipei, Taiwan. This little lady was known to many as "Typhoon Lil." She was an indefatigable worker among the Taiwanese, founding a number of leprosaria and ministering among the poorest of the poor in that struggling nation. She founded a work known as The Mustard Seed with headquarters in Glendale, California, but spent her adult life on the field in her ministry of mercy. It seemed as though she never slept, was constantly on the go, and ministered so lovingly to the hurting people on what was then known as Formosa. I was privileged on numerous occasions to visit various leprosy centers which she founded and which World Vision assisted in financial report. She was an unforgettable personality who is now with the Lord.

The third woman was Miss Irene Webster-Smith, a British lady who ministered in Tokyo. Probably in the post-war years no individual Christian made a more significant impact in evangelism than this dear lady. She was the founder, among other things, of the Tokyo Christian Student Center, a splendid three-story building in the heart of Tokyo which has housed numerous evangelical agency offices. Again, this lady impressed me with her zeal, her loving concern for the people of Japan and her strong evangelistic enterprises.

In 1966 the World Congress on Evangelism held in Berlin, co-sponsored by *Christianity Today* magazine and the Billy Graham Evangelistic Association, was a highlight of the decade. Along with several colleagues from World Vision, I was privileged to attend this most significant event. Official delegates from all across the world—Asia, Africa, Latin America and North America—shared in the eight days in West Berlin, listening to the outstanding messages from God's servants from across the globe. The Congress was indeed a defining moment in world evangelism later spawning similar congresses in Minneapolis, Singapore and elsewhere across the globe.

As an interesting sideline to the congress, one evening Bob Pierce and I invited a number of key leaders to be our guests at a special small, private dinner at the hotel where we were staying. Among these special guests was Oral Roberts, founder and speaker on a national radio and television program, an evangelist, "faith healer," and Pentecostal leader.

During the course of our dinner, Oral learned that I was having great difficulty with my hip, which I had injured in the jeep accident during my army days. He asked if it might be possible for him to pray for me about the pain with which I was struggling.

I was reluctant to do so, but my colleague Larry Ward strongly urged that I permit Oral Roberts to lay hands on me and pray for healing. My friends gathered around me as I knelt by the chair. Dr. Roberts did pray and as he laid hands on my hip, in his typical fashion, he prayed, "Lord—Heal, heal!" I was obviously nervous about this particular situation, but was deeply appreciative of his concern for me.

Nothing happened immediately as a result of that prayer time but two or three years later I went to Boston, Massachusetts, to the Massachusetts General Hospital for a hip replacement, which, I'm grateful to say, was successful.

Several years later, I was visiting on the campus of Oral Roberts University in Tulsa, Oklahoma and Oral Roberts heard that I was there and asked that I come to visit him for a time of fellowship and a cup of tea. Later that afternoon I did go up to his home close to the campus and had a happy time of renewed fellowship. In the course of our conversation, Oral asked me, "Ted, how's your health and your hip?"

I said, "Oral, how in the world did you remember that problem?"

"I do recall so clearly our prayer time in Berlin," Oral said, "and I'm just wondering how you are doing now."

I told him of the surgery experience in Massachusetts and that I was doing quite well with the injured hip. Oral responded, "Praise the Lord. God uses surgeons and modern medicine as part of His healing process, and God has answered our prayers." To me, it was interesting that he had recalled that event of some years prior.

It was to the 1966 Congress in Berlin that Rachel Saint, sister of Nate Saint, martyred by the Auca Indians in Ecuador, brought a group of converted Auca Indians. These three Indians had

Soon to be Mr. & Mrs. Engstrom, just prior to wedding, standing outside Taylor University in Upland, Indiana— Ted & Dorothy's Alma Mater.

In 1945, at the age of 29, Ted was the Editor of "Torney Topics" an Army newspaper.

Taken at the first citywide Billy Graham Crusade in Grand Rapids, where Ted was crusade director. From Left: Jack Sonneveldt, Ted, Billy Graham.

Ted and Jack Sonneveldt conduct a radio interview with Billy Graham during the Grand Rapids Crusade.

Ted and Bob Pierce stand for a picture with President Thieu in Saigon, Viet Nam.

The Masai people of Kenya respond with great success to World Vision's training program in agriculture.

Ted always enjoyed time spent with the Christian community in Kenya.

A surprise for Ted...when the front of the remote orphanage in Mali, Africa came into view, its name had a familiar ring!

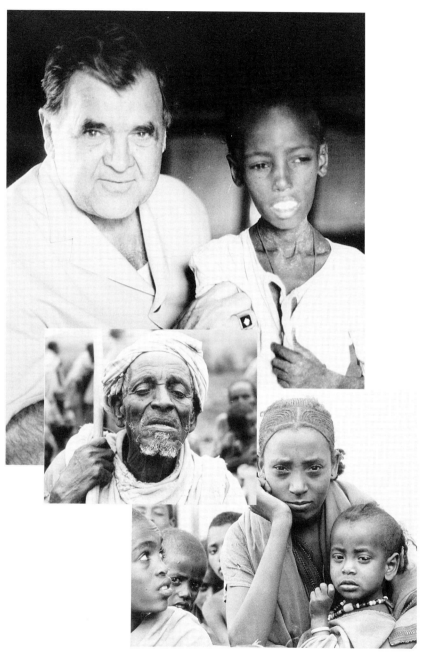

The years of famine in Ethiopia will forever be embedded in the minds of Americans who watched the disaster on TV. The unrelenting drought created starvation conditions for many Ethiopians. The severity of the famine convinced the Socialist government to give World Vision a free hand reaching out to the people with food and clothing and shelter.

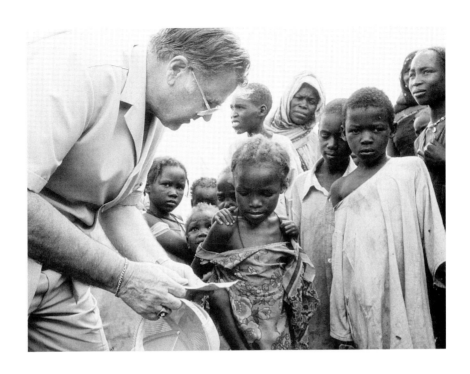

In Sudan, another famine brings the relief efforts of World Vision.

Mother Theresa met with Dr. Engstrom and Dr. Charles Blair, then pastor of the large Calvary Temple in Denver. Dr. Engstrom was very interested in her work in Calcutta and Mother Theresa was equally interested in the work of World Vision.

"Shoe shine, Mister?" After several deferrals, Dr. Ted finally relented and let the lad shine his shoes. Quick to secure ongoing business, Dwarka Das said, "I shine your shoes everyday!" Dr. Engstrom allowed Dwarka to shine his already shiny shoes each day and encouraged him to attend the evangelical church around the corner from his place of business. Within a few days, Dwarka gave his heart to Jesus Christ!

As Chairman of the English Language Institute/China, Dr. Engstrom was given direct access to students while placing English teachers in Chinese Universities.

English Language Institute/China enjoyed the same success in Tibet by placing English teachers in the University. Here is the largest monastery in the world—the 999 room Buddhist monastery in Lhasa, Tibet, at 12,336 feet above sea level, the highest capital in the world.

Lady Gladys Donnithorne, a member of the British Aristocracy, was an example to everyone. Here she is receiving a plaque of recognition for her endless and joy-filled work among the poor of Hong Kong. Even though born to wealth and position, she devoted her life to meeting needs and testifying to Christ in the then filthy, disease ridden back streets of Hong Kong—in those days known as the other "Forbidden City."

World Vision sponsored the Korean Children's Choir. Dr. Engstrom often traveled with them and shared a special relationship with many of the children.

Everyone knew her as "Typhoon Lil" Dickson—a remarkable Christian lady. Her energy was boundless. She rarely slept. She was a most indefatigable missionary and played a key role for the Kingdom in the post war years in Taiwan.

Ted and Sylvia Nash, CEO of Christian Management Association, take a moment to talk with CMA keynote speaker, Peter Drucker.

The year was 1974. Bringing the plight of may people to a western audience was often dangerous. Here Ted leans over a machine gun mounted on the helicopter, pausing for a picture with a film crew in Cambodia.

Dr. Engstrom with Hall of Fame basketball coach (perhaps the greatest basketball coach of all time) John Wooden of UCLA.

Dr. Engstrom with famed music conductor and friend, Ralph Carmichael.

Having fun! Ted is asked to announce the start of the Great American Cross-Country Auto Race. Before the race gets started, Ted has a moment to speak with baseball star Jose Cruz.

The Ted Engstrom family today. Regrettably, Gordon's wife, Lynn, was out of the country at the time this picture was taken.

never been out of the jungle prior to that experience and seeing elevators, escalators, and hotel beds was all strange to them. They had come out of what was practically a stone age to the twentieth century by means of an air flight overnight!

It was marvelous to hear their simple testimony of the grace of God in their lives and how, although they had killed the five missionaries in 1955, they were now serving the one living God. In addition, an Auca lady named Dayuma was introduced by Rachel Saint as the first convert in the Auca tribe. What a warm welcome was received by these Indians from the delegates of the Congress from all across the globe.

——— ——— ———

In 1968 the Billy Graham Evangelistic Association also sponsored a Congress in Singapore titled "The Asia, South Pacific Congress on Evangelism." Twenty-five nations from Asia were represented. Half of the delegates were laymen and eighty percent were from these Asian nations. The theme selected was "Christ Seeks Asia," and the impact was felt in church growth and evangelism throughout all of southeast Asia in the following years. It was a pleasure for me to be a special invited guest at this significant and meaningful conclave.

——— ——— ———

At this time I was continuing to have considerable painful problems with my hip. World Vision kindly granted me a six-week leave of absence to go, with Dorothy, to the Massachusetts General Hospital for my hip replacement, which, as indicated, was eminently successful. It was wonderful during those days to have many special friends in New England to visit with me in the hospital. These included Dr. Harold Ockenga from Gordon Conwell Seminary; Dr. Paul Toms, pastor of the Park Street Church in Boston; John Debrine, a pastor friend in the Boston area; Dr. Bob Cook, who drove up from King's College in Briarcliffe Manor in New York, and many others.

——— ——— ———

During the very difficult period of working with Dr. Pierce prior to his resignation of the World Vision presidency, I told my beloved friend Dr. Dick Halverson, chairman of our board, that I was leaving my post at World Vision, having been invited to go back to a senior post at the Zondervan Publishing House.

"Ted, you can't leave." Dick said to me as we chatted in the parking lot of the World Vision building.

"Of course I can," I responded."

"No—you can't."

"Why not? I'm a free agent, I can do as I wish."

"Do you want to be a murderer?" Dick asked.

"Of course not," I replied. "What do you mean?"

"If you leave now you will kill the organization."

Certainly that was very much an overstatement, but the Lord used that conversation to hold me steady at my post at World Vision, for which I have been forever grateful. Dick Halverson was a very special colleague whom I valued as a close brother in Christ.

The pressures of the work of World Vision and his intense involvement with suffering people across the world affected Bob Pierce physically, emotionally and psychologically. In 1967 the board of World Vision urged Bob to take a lengthy leave of absence from the leadership of the organization. He did so for a period of eight or nine months, the first of which he spent in a psychiatric clinic in Switzerland, where seemingly after many days of "deep sleep treatment" he seemed to be a changed individual. Later during this period he spent several months in retreat in Japan.

Bob came back to his position at World Vision for a year but was unable to cope with the pressures, and finally, at the request of the board, resigned his leadership role. It was at this time that Dick Halverson served as interim president and I with him as executive vice president. Shortly thereafter we began our search for the second president of World Vision.

As a result of having a summer cottage at the Maranatha Bible Conference on Lake Michigan, I arranged for World Vision to sponsor a week of missions at the conference for a number of summers in this decade. We invited top national leaders from across the world to share in the speaking ministry, along with missionary leaders from North America. The large tabernacle at Maranatha was filled nightly during that missions emphasis week and great enthusiasm was engendered for the cause of missions and the particular role that God had given to World Vision in evangelism, relief and development ministries. As a result, Western Michigan became one of the key supporting areas for the World Vision program.

My family and I have very fond memories of our experiences at the Maranatha Bible Conference. I was asked to serve on the board with Howard Skinner, the General Director of the conference and did so with delight for many years. Choice friends who had property on the Conference grounds comprised the board which worked with the Director in the three month Bible conference programming. The services held morning and evening throughout the entire summer were enriching, inspiring and immensely helpful. Some of the finest Bible teachers in the country shared in the ministry and our hosting many of them at our cottage following an evening service was a particular delight for Dorothy and me. And, having our children under the strong teaching and biblical influence of the summer program was most meaningful—both to us as parents and to them as our children.

Following Bob Pierce's resignation from the presidency of World Vision in 1968, three of us—Dick Halverson, Paul Rees and I—went to Singapore to interview a very special individual, Dr. Stan Mooneyham, regarding the possibility of his becoming the second president of World Vision. I had known Stan for a number of years through his leadership with the National Association of Evangelicals, the Evangelical Press Association and the Billy Graham Evangelistic Association—as well as being a neighbor in Wheaton earlier on.

The committee came back to the World Vision board with the strong recommendation that Stan be invited to be our president. He was just finishing his key responsibility as director of the

Asia/South Pacific Congress on Evangelism in Singapore. Following a time of seeking counsel and prayer, Stan did, gratefully, accept the invitation of the World Vision board to come with us as our president, with my continuing to work along side of him as the executive vice president. (More of this in succeeding chapters.)

———————

As Dorothy, the family and I moved to California earlier on, we asked the Lord for His guidance regarding what church to associate with and to join. God graciously guided us to the large, warm, evangelical Lake Avenue Congregational Church, in Pasadena, pastored by my special friend Dr. Ray Ortlund. It has been a wonderful experience over the years to have shared in the fellowship of the church and to have served in practically every office, including twice being the church chairman or moderator.

Soon after my arrival at Lake Avenue, Ray Ortlund and I determined to form a small accountability group to meet for breakfast on a monthly basis. We invited four colleagues, not all from the same church, to join with us in this fellowship which continued meeting for almost twenty–five years with, obviously, some changes in individuals with whom I had the joy of meeting and holding myself accountable in my walk with the Lord. The Lake Avenue Church has formed a strong foundation for the family and me for over all these years for which I am most grateful indeed.

One of the memorable experiences following our move from Wheaton to Arcadia, California, was a special and unique ministry among our new neighbors. One day Dorothy was shopping in the local market when she met a lady who was a neighbor, Bette Vessey. The two struck up an acquaintance and Dorothy indicated that she would like to know Bette as a friend and neighbor and invited her over to our home for a cup of coffee and fellowship.

A few days later Bette did drop by and in their conversation she indicated to Dorothy that although they were a family of considerable means they had deep needs spiritually. Dorothy indicated that it would be great if she, her husband, Ned, and we could meet together for a time of sharing.

About that same time, our daughter JoAnn met a lovely little girl in her grade school and invited her to a slumber party at our home. Janet's mother, Betty Hawkins, visited our home before her daughter came up for that night with us. Betty's husband, Herb, was and is a prominent real estate entrepreneur in Southern California with several dozen real estate offices which he owned and operated. Again, a warm friendship began with the Hawkins family.

A bit later we had plans to attend a Layman's Leadership Institute at the Broadmoor Hotel in Colorado Springs. A friend suggested that perhaps these two new couples whom we had met, both of whom had spiritual needs, could possibly accompany us to this special layman's outreach. Both couples were willing to join with us and so the six of us traveled to the three-day conference which was addressed by key Christian lay leaders such as Howard Butt, Jr., Fred Smith, Sr. and others. The Lord wonderfully worked in the lives of these four new friends and on the closing session on a Sunday morning, addressed by Howard Butt, all four of these people committed their lives to Christ.

This began a wonderful experience in our neighborhood. The six of us determined that we would invite our neighbors in for evening dessert times for what we would call a Neighborhood Christian Round Table. Over the next weeks and months we held numerous of these evenings with our neighbor guests discussing such things as "raising teenagers in today's society," and seeking to find answers in the "world's best seller," and "How to hold high standards in our business and community relationships." As a result of these sessions over the months, a score or more of these neighbors/friends came to faith in Jesus Christ and the friendships have continued through the years.

All five of the Vessey young adult children came to faith as did the two fine children of the Hawkins, several of whom are in Christian ministry and all of whom are active in their local churches.

Not long after we came to Pasadena, I was invited to share in the early days of a ministry known as African Enterprise. AE, as it has been known, was founded by a young Fuller Seminary student by the name of Michael Cassidy. Michael was converted as a university student, from South Africa, while at Cambridge University in England, largely under the influence of Billy Graham. He came to Pasadena as a student at Fuller and was burdened for evangelism in the cities of Africa. Through the encouragement of Dr. Charles Fuller and people like faculty member Carlton Booth and a fine businessman named Bruce Bare, he organized a small board in 1963 legally established as African Enterprise, Inc. I was asked to join the board and happily did so.

This became one of the delights and joys of my experience. Michael and his team of young men began to hold evangelistic campaigns in practically all of the major capitals of the fifty-plus nations in Africa with significant results. Over the years he became a confidant to the political leaders of South Africa and was instrumental ultimately in the dismantling of the tragic apartheid situation which tragically marked that nation.

Over the ensuing years, it was my privilege to visit with Mike and the team on numerous occasions in South Africa, including participating in a great African Congress on Evangelism held in Durban, South Africa. In addition, I have visited the team's headquarters in Pietermaritzburg on numerous occasions. Indeed, one of the most significant ministries being conducted in Africa over nearly forty years has come about through the influence of the African Enterprise teams. Having been a member of the AE Board for all these years, on separate occasions I've had the privilege of serving as its chairman with some wonderfully dedicated and gifted people.

Shortly after arriving in Southern California, Dorothy and I were invited to participate in the dedication of the new headquarters for Campus Crusade for Christ at Arrowhead Springs. CCC had purchased a beautiful resort hotel there at a bargain rate together with property which became one of the key and most beautiful Christian conference centers in the state.

The speaker for that special occasion was Dr. Waiter Judd, a former medical missionary to China and a congressman from Minnesota. What excitement surrounded that special occasion with hosts of Christian leaders from Southern California who joined in the time of celebration and dedication with my special friend Dr. Bill Bright and his staff, which had grown sizably over the recent years, both in numbers and in influence.

Through my warm friendship with Russ Reid, a former Youth for Christ director and then the sales manager for Word Records in Waco, Texas, I was introduced to a gentleman who became a warm friend, Jarrell McCracken, president of Word Records, Inc. Jarrell had decided to enlarge his business from sacred recordings to the publishing of Christian books and asked if I would be willing to serve on the board of this new organization to be known as Word Books, Incorporated. Along with Stan Mooneyham, Russ Reid, Ken Anderson and others, I did serve on the board with great delight. As a matter of fact, I was asked to edit the first book that Word Books ever published—a book by Keith Miller entitled *A Taste of New Wine* which became a national bestseller. The association I had with Word over the years was a delight, and friendships formed during those days in the 60s have remained.

It was during this decade that my friend Sam Moore, President of Thomas Nelson Publishers in Nashville, Tennessee, whom I had gotten to know over the years, invited me to Nashville to explore the possibility of becoming president of that fine organization. I visited Thomas Nelson on two occasions, but did not feel that moving there was the Lord's leading, although I have always had a warm appreciation for Christian book publishing. Over the years I have had the privilege of having a number of my books published by Thomas Nelson, who later had Here's Life Publishers and Word Books merge with them, both of which had published books of mine.

During the decade of the 60s I was invited to share as a member of the board of trustees of a fine Quaker school in Newberg, Oregon, George Fox College. Dr. David LeShana was the president of the college at that time and through his invitation I served on the board of GFC for a number of years, forming friendships and being able to share my enthusiasm for Christian higher education. Dr. LeShana later became president at Seattle Pacific University and during his tenure there I was invited to give the commencement address and also receive an honorary LL.D.degree.

At a conference for Christian leaders conducted in the late 60s at Glen Eyrie, Colorado, the headquarters for the Navigators, I had the privilege of meeting one of the officers of the American Management Association, Alec Mackenzie, a fine, committed Christian. While together there he and I discussed the possibility of writing a book jointly on a theme which keenly interested us both—the management of time. We decided to collaborate on such a book which later was published by Zondervan entitled *Managing Your Time*, which over the years has become a bestseller. It also became the first of a sizable series of management and leadership books I had the privilege of authoring, and having published.

Though it was a time of real spiritual and professional growth for me, the 60s had a certain uneasiness about it that always seemed to lurk in the background. This decade began with a strong sense of uncertainty about our economy, the nation's moral deterioration and an uneasy discomfort about our future. It closed with a continuing deep feeling of apprehension about the years to come. Yet for the believer there seemed to be a fresh recognition of God's working in His Church, including significant growth in a host of parachurch ministries, which continued into the next decade.

"This was a rock-throwing, flag-burning, draft-card destroying time of protest.

…there was a renewed sense of optimism in many areas related to the Church and evangelism. There seemed to be a "ying-yang" effect across the nation—a host of problems, and alongside them many events by which believers were spiritually renewed and in which we rejoiced."

4

REFLECTIONS

The 1970s – The Decade of Disillusionment

IF THE DECADE OF THE 60S WAS MARKED BY REBEL-
lion, the decade that followed, according to my special friend Bill
Hybels, was one of disillusionment. I fully agree with Bill.

The 1960s had witnessed three devastating assassinations:
John Kennedy, Martin Luther King, Jr., and Robert Kennedy.
Hopes were dashed as each of these men of promise and vision
was wiped out by an assassin's bullet.

Four key events of the 70s led to our national disillusionment: the Vietnam war; Watergate and President Nixon's eventual resignation; the oil price wars and gas shortages; and finally,
the Jimmy Carter presidency which faced a backlog of unsolved
problems related to economics, hostages, oil shortages, moral
relevancy and despondency.

At the dawn of the 1970s gasoline sold for 35 cents a gallon
and gold was priced officially at $35 an ounce. At the end of the

decade we were paying 300 percent more for gasoline and an ounce of gold was traded for nearly 1,300 percent more per ounce.

In May 1971, frightened, young, nervous National Guardsmen foolishly opened fire on Kent State University students in Kent, Ohio, killing four and wounding ten. This singular event characterized the larger sense of a decade of hate-filled protests and deep fears among polarized sides. This was a rock-throwing, flag-burning, draft-card destroying time of protest.

As we shall note, however, there was a renewed sense of optimism in many areas related to the Church and evangelism. There seemed to be a "ying-yang" effect across the nation—a host of problems, and alongside them many events by which believers were spiritually renewed and in which we rejoiced.

The decade of the 70s began with the U.S. still at war in Vietnam, but with hosts of our young people protesting and burning American flags in the streets. Huge numbers of them were involved in radical left politics, free sex, drugs and other moral problems. An entire generation seemed to be lost.

Early in 1973 the Supreme Court ruled that a state may not prevent a woman from getting an abortion during the first six months of pregnancy and issued the infamous Roe vs. Wade decision, which ever since has affected our national political scene. A year later President Nixon resigned in disgrace, and Vice President Gerald Ford succeeded him.

By the end of the decade our world population had passed four billion, the U.S. population topped 220 million and California surpassed New York's eighteen and a half million population for the first time.

On the international front, from 1975 to 1978 an estimated one million people were murdered in Cambodia due to the repressive Killing Fields, a warped and evil mentality of the Khmer Rouge government. By 1979 Vietnam invaders had captured the capital, Phnom Penh, at least diminishing the traumas on the gentle Cambodian people.

China, a seemingly hopeless ideological recluse among major nations, opened its door a crack in 1971 when President Richard Nixon visited that nation. In 1979 full diplomatic recognition was given by the U.S. and the door seemed to open to some new spiritual approaches from Christians as well.

In 1976 *Christianity Today* magazine called that year "The Year of the Evangelical" as evangelicals were estimated to number in the tens of millions in the U.S. President Carter is also credited during this period with helping to raise the spiritual and moral consciousness of many in the country. Evangelicals were viewed increasingly as not just reactionary, but of vigorously and sometimes creatively speaking to the needs of the contemporary society. A bit later *Time* magazine picked up this theme as well.

It was early in this decade that *Look* magazine featured the Jesus Movement as young people hit the streets, parks and beaches with guitars and Bibles in an outpouring of witness that was related to the times and culture. There were Jesus music concerts, Jesus tabloids and Jesus witness marches, as well as Christian coffee houses and hotline ministries. These new converts were urged to be grounded in Scripture and to join a Christian fellowship. This marked the beginning of the Calvary Chapel movement, led by pastor Chuck Smith in Costa Mesa, California, which rapidly spread across the nation. By the middle of the decade, Pastor Smith's congregation had grown from a handful to over 15,000 young people under the age of thirty-five.

The Jesus Movement spread rapidly, emerging from the debris of Haight-Ashbury in San Francisco, Sunset Strip in Hollywood, and a dozen other unlikely places. These youthful Christians came bounding into the decade with joy, enthusiasm, love for others, and unabashed openness in sharing Christ.

In 1976 Russian moralist, writer and speaker, Alexandar Solzhenitsyn, a Nobel Prize winner, gave an address at Harvard University commencement entitled "A World Split Apart" in which he indicated that not only Russian society, but Western society as well, was morally impoverished and questioned our materialism, our manipulation of the law, and our lack of political courage.

In 1972 Campus Crusade for Christ sponsored a large and

significant conference of young people known as Expo '72 in Dallas, Texas. The mass meetings were held in the large Cotton Bowl stadium with over 70,000 youth in attendance. Paul Eshleman, on the Campus Crusade staff, gave direction to Expo '72 and on the closing evening, when Billy Graham gave the address, all 70,000 participants lighted candles in a darkened stadium. It was a thrilling evangelistic event and an unforgettable sight to me. Each day of the conference was spent in discipleship training for these tens of thousands of key college and university students. Out of this meeting came the Campus Crusade "Here's life" and "I Found It" evangelistic campaigns which swept the nation.

Early in the 70s Youth with a Mission and other groups spearheaded coast-to-coast witnessing in connection with the nation's upcoming bicentennial, and 17,000 students flocked to Urbana, Illinois, for InterVarsity's Triennial Student Missionary Convention.

The conversion in 1973 of Watergate figure Charles Colson, who became a dear friend of mine, and then the candidacy of born-again Governor Jimmy Carter of Georgia for President in 1976, landed the Gospel on page one of our newspapers. Books like Colson's *Born Again* and Hal Lindsey's *The Late Great Planet Earth* helped make the 1970s a boon for evangelical publishing.

Christian radio was bigger than ever, and Christian television stations—served by communication satellites in space—were being established at the rate of one a month at the end of the decade.

An event close to me personally occurred in 1968 when Bob Pierce formed a fine organization which he entitled Samaritan's Purse, a practical service agency to missionaries and key national leaders, primarily across Asia. Prior to his death in 1978, Bob turned this ministry over to Franklin Graham, the son of Billy Graham. Under Franklin's guidance and direction this ministry has expanded greatly in influence and effectiveness over the years.

It's regrettable that, during the last decade of his life, Bob Pierce was separated from his family. There was no divorce but he and the family did not live together, which caused great pain to both Bob and Mrs. Pierce and the children. Just days before Bob went to be with the Lord he invited his wife Lorraine and his daughters Marilee and Robin, together with their husbands, to have a dinner with him in a downtown Los Angeles hotel. By all accounts it was a very meaningful time of reconciliation prior to Bob's homegoing. Earlier on, most regrettably, his eldest daughter Sharon, in the midst of a great deal of personal trauma, had taken her life, which obviously shattered Bob and the family.

——— ——— ———

Toward the end of the decade large numbers of Christians became involved for the first time in grass roots politics, through such groups as the Moral Majority, headed up by Reverend Jerry Falwell, Evangelicals for Social Action, led by Ron Sider, and the Bread for the World movement.

——— ——— ———

A key event in the ongoing history of World Vision occurred in 1978 when we as an organization decided to "internationalize." Stan Mooneyham had the burden—in light of the formation of dozens of national entities in World Vision, both support and field—to establish a structure allowing these entities to have an equal voice in the ministries that we jointly represented. Thus, in 1977 he invited key leaders in World Vision from across the world to meet at Pattaya Beach in Thailand for a week of preliminary discussion and to brainstorm this potential new organizational concept and how it might affect each of the core entities. Meeting with us were special counselors such as Senator Mark Hatfield and some key mission leaders, not only from America but from other parts of the world.

A year later a larger group of us met at the Kahala Hilton Hotel in Honolulu and for a second week crafted the details of what this new organization might be. Under our new structure, the original World Vision entity, headquartered in America, gave up much of its authority to the new World Vision International office, which also would be located in Southern California but in a separate building. My colleague, Graeme Irvine, was charged with the responsibility to implement the internationalization document which was developed at the Hawaii meeting. This effort of internationalization proved to be a model for many other international organizations and they have, over the years, studied the process of allowing separate country entities to have a strong voice in policy matters related to the ministry. Initially, there were approximately thirty entities which formed the international organism. Over the years that has grown to over sixty separate national members.

At first, Stan Mooneyham served as the president of both World Vision U.S. and World Vision International, while I continued to serve as the executive vice president for both organizations as well. When Stan resigned some years later, I followed in his footsteps as president of both the U.S. and International organizations until 1984, when the Reverend Tom Houston, from the British Bible Society, was invited to become the International president. Thus released from leading the International entity, I continued as president of the U.S. support office. This move to internationalization was one of the most significant events in the almost fifty-year history of World Vision.

———

Without doubt, I believe the most important event for evangelicals in the world in 1974 was the International Congress on World Evangelism held in Lausanne, Switzerland. There were 4,000 attendees for the week-long conference from 150 nations and five continents. The movers and shakers in our evangelical world were there, representing scores of denominations and parachurch groups, as well as key pastors and laymen.

The congress was a follow-up to the Berlin Congress on Evangelism held in 1966, with the further theme of banding together in the common task of world evangelization. A key document was developed during the long late hours of the conference in what has been described as the Lausanne Covenant. A committee, chaired by Dr. John Stott, Rector of the All Soul's

Anglican Church in London and a highly appreciated and regarded international churchman, developed the document. It was strongly debated in plenary sessions of the congress by the official delegates but was ultimately adopted. The Covenant has proved to be a key statement related to the task of the Church in the last decades of the twentieth century related to the fulfilling of our Lord's Great Commission.

Billy Graham served as the honorary chairman of the congress and my friend Don Hoke, president of a Christian college in Tokyo at that time, was the conference director. It was a personal pleasure for me to meet and greet so many individuals whom I had known over the years and to have the renewed fellowship with friends from across Europe, Africa, Asia and Latin America.

It was during this period that I invited my very close friends Herb and Betty Hawkins to accompany Dorothy and me on a ministry trip around the world. I had invited Herb to become a member of our board of World Vision and we were having the special conference related to internationalization in Thailand. We were eager for Herb and Betty to share this experience with us.

En route to Thailand we stopped for two or three days in Athens and then for a day or two in northern India, where the Hawkins visited the famed Taj Mahal. Following our time in Thailand we visited the World Vision ministries in Seoul, Korea, where we were hosted by the vice prime minister at a lovely banquet reception in the Blue House, next to the residence of the president of the country. Our Korean hosts were most generous in their appreciation for what World Vision had done since the early 1950s in alleviating the suffering in their nation.

Early in the 1970s Stan Mooneyham conducted two significant evangelistic crusades in Phnom Penh, the capital of Cambodia. That country has historically been a Buddhist stronghold with a minimum Christian witness.

When Stan and a colleague drove a truckload of medical supplies, on a dangerous war-torn route between Saigon, Vietnam and Phnom Penh, he won the favor of the Cambodian leadership and was granted permission to conduct evangelistic meetings, each day late in the afternoon for a week, in a large public hall in the center of the capital city. I was privileged to be with him in the first of these campaigns and saw literally hundreds of Cambodian men and women, as well as young people, take a stand for Christ. The meetings were a tremendous encouragement to the struggling evangelical church movement in the country and enabled the churches to grow sizeable as a result.

Later, permission was granted to World Vision to build and staff the first Christian children's hospital in the nation. The project was headed up by World Vision board member Winston Weaver, a beloved friend, from Harrisonburg, Virginia.

With the fall of the government to the Pol Pot regime in 1975 the hospital was closed, taken over by the insurgents and sadly became a torture chamber for those opposed to the Pol Pot government.

Thousands of refugees left the country in the late 1970s and literally hundreds of thousands of those unsympathetic to the new government were cruelly murdered. Tragically, included in this number was our faithful World Vision Cambodian director.

Following the fall of South Vietnam to the Communist regime from the North, tens of thousands of Vietnamese from the South sought to escape from the nation by means of small seacrafts, often unseaworthy, down the Mekong River and into the South China Sea. As a result of the high number of refugee deaths in the treacherous ocean, World Vision purchased a large freighter from a firm in Australia and equipped it to patrol the waters of the South China Sea to pick up these boat refugees by the hundreds. A crew to man the boat, named *Sea Sweep*, was brought together under the leadership of a naval veteran from World Vision, Burt Singleton.

On one occasion, off the shore of Malaysia, Dorothy and I were privileged to board the ship and visit with 150 or more of these refugees who had just been picked up out of the sea and brought to safety. Many of them were brought into a camp in Singapore, others to Malaysia and still others to Thailand. All were then brought, via Hong Kong, either to Europe or America. The *Sea Sweep* adventure was a risky, but eminently worthwhile saga in the World Vision history during this decade.

Toward the close of the decade the explosive growth of the Chinese Church was becoming increasingly apparent, with reports of tens of millions of Chinese coming to believing faith, especially through the house church movement all across the nation. It was estimated that there were a maximum of three million believers, both Roman Catholic and Protestant, in China when it fell to the Communists in 1949-50, and near the end of this century there are an estimated forty to fifty million believers in the People's Republic, with evidence of continued dramatic growth in succeeding years.

The American mood towards China began to change early in the 70s when President Nixon made his unprecedented historic visit to this Communist nation. Later that same year Nixon visited Moscow and had his confrontation and a test of wills with the Russian President.

One of the ventures that marked World Vision during the 70s was the inauguration of various kinds of television programming. Stan Mooneyham had a deep concern for the use of this media and handled it wisely, professionally, and with integrity.

We also inaugurated a series of two thirteen week, thirty minute telecasts which we entitled *Come Walk the World*. In this program, Stan served as the host and we had filmed reports from the World Vision ministry all across the world. It proved to be a venture of faith, seeking to challenge Christians to a more compassionate worldview, and God honored it with a strong response from viewers across the nation.

In addition World Vision sponsored one–hour, two–hour and three–hour telethons, usually focusing on hunger and displaced peoples, with phone call-ins from listeners. It proved, often with graphic and realistic footage, the old adage of a picture being worth a thousand words, and enhanced the scope and breadth of our ministry. On these programs we had key guests who endorsed with great feeling this ministry of mercy across the globe. Included were such well–known personalities as Art Linkletter, Bob Hope, President Gerald Ford, Julie Andrews, Alec Trebak and hosts of others.

Television specials helped our World Vision ministry to expand in unprecedented ways, gave us a high profile across the nation, and elevated the witness of Christians to a lost and suffering world in the minds of hosts of individuals.

Children have always held a place of high honor in World Vision, including orphans and needy children from Korea, some of whom had exceptional talents in music.

Our World Vision-sponsored Korean Children's Choir had many memorable experiences as they traveled across the United States and Canada. One of the highlights was a concert appearance, in which I also participated, at the Kennedy Center in Washington, D.C. The junior senator from Virginia was our host for this very special black-tie occasion. The children were accompanied by a full philharmonic orchestra and performed beautifully. We had a reception for our special guests following the concert, and I recall the privilege of meeting the famed baseball star Mickey Mantle at this after-concert gathering.

One of the personal highlights for me in this decade of the 70s was sharing in pastors' conferences sponsored by World Vision across the globe, initially with my beloved friend Dr. Paul Rees and then later with my colleague, Dr. Sam Kamaleson.

Memorable conferences with Dr. Rees and the team were conducted in Quito, Ecuador, where over 300 national pastors met with us; in Guadalajara, Mexico, again with several hundred Christian workers sharing; and in Puna, India, at the Seventh Day Adventist College, again with over 400 ministers who were encouraged and challenged to follow Christ more faithfully in the four-day training conference.

Late in the decade I was privileged to share with Sam Kamaleson and his team in places like Fiji; Bangalor, India; Sao Paulo, Brazil; Madras, India; Hong Kong, and Barbados in the Caribbean. In each of these venues we experienced warm friendship with national leaders and saw God move in a remarkable fashion through the leadership of team members such as Dick Halverson, Dr. Han from Korea and Carl F.H. Henry, together with many national leaders from across the globe who were invited to be equal partners on the speaking team with Dr. Rees and Dr. Kamaleson.

These were unforgettable experiences in meeting some of God's choicest and self-sacrificing servants, and I am immensely grateful for being a part of this ministry to national Christian leaders which God blessed so richly through the World Vision sponsorship.

My young friend Preston Hawkins was, during this time, just beginning his career in real estate with his father, my special friend, Herb Hawkins. Preston accompanied me on a series of pastor's conferences in Latin America led by Dr. Rees. We were together in a very unusual conference high in the Andes in Quito, followed by time in Guatemala City just after the gigantic earthquake it had suffered, and then in Guadalajara. Preston has indicated on numerous occasions the spiritual impact he sensed as a result of sharing in these deeply spiritual training sessions with Christian leaders in the Third World context.

⸻

On one of my frequent visits to Korea I was invited by the president of the nation to participate in a ceremony in the Blue House, similar to our Washington White House. On behalf of the numerous World Vision staff, I and three others representing sister agencies were given the Order of Civil Merit, the highest civilian award for non-Koreans, in appreciation of the work being carried on in that nation by our organizations. It was a most impressive, solemn occasion—one which I will never forget. Following the formal presentation there was a reception where we were able to meet many of the top leadership people in the government, a number of whom were believers.

On one of the first of my many visits to South Vietnam in the 70s, I was introduced to a wonderful gentleman who became a great friend. General Khang Le and his wife Thu became very dear to Dorothy and me. General Khang was Commandant of the South Vietnamese Marine Corps and just prior to the fall of the capital, Saigon, in 1975, was Governor of Saigon Province. When we dedicated the first building of World Vision in Saigon, Thu Le, who was a member of what was known as the General's Wives Organization, cut the ribbon for the opening of our new facility. Her husband was a confirmed Buddhist but she had been trained in a Catholic high school.

The general was keenly interested in the work and ministry of World Vision and helped us in innumerable ways with our program. On occasion he would assign one of his helicopters to us to visit our various projects across the war-torn nation. At other times he would make his vehicles available for use in the city.

I recall on one occasion when we were on one of the Marine Corps helicopters visiting a U.S. Army outpost where a hundred or more of our troops were on the frontline and in extreme danger. Nearby was an orphanage that World Vision sponsored which we wanted to visit. The building had been evacuated and the children taken elsewhere but we could see evidences of the bullet holes that had wracked the building. My neighbor friend, Ned Vessey, and our World Vision International vice president Larry Ward and I made this eventful trip behind the lines—such as they were—in South Vietnam.

The General and his family were evacuated by U.S. forces out of Saigon during the last hours before the city fell to the Communists. A day or two earlier, Mrs. Le and the three children were evacuated and eventually brought to a Vietnamese refugee center in Arkansas. Later, during the last hours before Saigon fell, the General was evacuated to Guam. Both the General and his family had my address and each contacted me in California, not knowing where the other parties were. Gratefully, I was able to put them in touch with each other and they were happily reunited some weeks later at Camp Pendleton in Southern California.

As they moved to California I was able to secure a position for the General with the County of Los Angeles through my friendship with County Supervisor Kenneth Hahn. Khang's role in the county government was to assist Vietnamese who had escaped from Southeast Asia under the oppression of the Communist regimes.

Dorothy and I were very close to the family and had invited them to attend services at our home church. One Sunday evening, following the service, we had the General and his wife come to our home for some dessert and coffee and in our discussion I asked them if they would like to invite the Lord Jesus Christ into their lives as Lord and Savior. Immediately they responded that this is what they wanted. We prayed together and it was a genuinely transforming experience for both of them. They became active in our local church and, until Khang's death in 1996, bore a strong witness among their Vietnamese colleagues.

The Le's children did not speak English when they came to America but all three were brilliant and graduated with honors from UCLA: the son, Lac, with an engineering degree; a daughter, Bobo, as a pharmacist; and the second daughter, Bebe, as an attorney. All are doing extremely well in their chosen professions.

While visiting with the General one time in his home in Saigon, I noticed his keen interest in spiritual matters. He had been reading Hal Lindsey's best selling book, *The Late Great Planet Earth* and was intrigued by the prophetic message. This engendered a number of conversations concerning Scripture, the return of Christ, and the fulfillment of prophecy. I'm sure this book by Lindsey had a profound impact upon the General as part of his eventual conversion experience.

The decade of the 70s, for me, marked a considerable number of trips to the continent of Africa, visiting such nations as Ghana, Kenya, Zimbabwe, Tanzania, Liberia, Mauritania, Senegal, Mali, Egypt and most significantly Ethiopia, which suffered such severe famine with the tragic deaths of thousands, largely children and women.

On most of these trips I had both World Vision colleagues and World Vision donors along with me, to minister to our World Vision staff, participate in strategic conferences, preach in churches in hosts of cities and villages, and frequently meet with government officials related to our programs. My administrative assistant, John Foulkes, accompanied me on a number of these trips and was tremendously helpful in making travel arrangements, hosting our guests and being a special aide-de-camp to me.

On one of my frequent visits during this period of time to East Africa, particularly to Kenya, my friend James Magaria, a key Christian lay leader and former Chief of Police of the city of Nairobi, invited me to meet with the President of Kenya, Daniel Arap Moi. James and I spent about forty-five minutes in the president's office detailing some of the ministries of World Vision. President Moi is a churchman, a believer, and very sympathetic to evangelism efforts. At the close of our conference together we asked if we might pray with him and for him. He was most pleased. Following time in his office he took us for a delightful walk through the gardens of his presidential estate outside Nairobi.

During this time Reverend Tom Houston, who later would be named president of world Vision International, was pastor of the large and effective Nairobi Baptist Church. One Sunday while I was worshipping with that congregation President Moi was a special invited guest. A newly printed edition of the Scriptures was presented to him in the service. He gave a clear witness of his faith in Christ at that time.

Some friends who shared in these trips included my Lake Avenue Congregational Church pastor, Dr. Paul Cedar; a warm friend and World Vision board member, Steve Lazarian, and his wife Iris; my friend Phil Harmon from Seattle; and Christian philanthropist Howard Ahmanson.

A special friendship formed from my several visits to Africa with Bishop Festo Kevengere, an Anglican bishop from the trouble nation of Uganda. Festo was both a gifted evangelist and administrator who became part of the African Enterprise team, headed up by Michael Cassidy, on which board I had served for many years.

Festo had watched as his good friend the Archbishop was assassinated by military forces of Idi Amin, Uganda's demonic dictator. Festo dared to stand before Amin and bravely spoke a prophetic word for Christ, holding Amin accountable for that cruel assassination. Festo then had to flee from Uganda by foot to neighboring Kenya. He had an amazing ministry across the globe.

I shared in numerous meetings, conferences and dinners with this special friend. I recall one memorable occasion when I hosted an African Enterprise donor dinner for Mike Cassidy and Festo as our special guests. I sat between the two of them on the dais and just before Mike got up to speak he leaned across me at the table and asked Festo if he could share his half-full glass of water. To me this was symbolic of reconciliation of black Africans and white Europeans sharing in a common Christian fellowship.

My sister Ruth and her husband, Ted Andrianoff, were for many years missionaries in Laos in Southeast Asia (Indochina). Ted became field director of the Christian & Missionary Alliance in that small tribal mountainous nation.

On one occasion on a visit to that part of the world, I was grateful for the opportunity to spend a couple of days with Ruth and Ted in their home among the Laotians and visit the Bible school where Ted was teaching.

Another friend from boyhood days, Ed Gustafsen, also a Christian & Missionary Alliance missionary, was stationed in Laos as well. Ed invited me to fly with him in an MAF single-engine airplane up to the Burmese border where we were hosted by a tribal chief. Ed was keenly interested in seeing a church planted in that area and discussed this possibility with the chief. It was fascinating to be in that thatched roof home talking about the Gospel to a person who probably had very little knowledge of what a church was or what we meant by the Good News of the Gospel. Later I learned that the Lord enabled Ed to plant a church in that area, known as the Golden Triangle where Laos, Burma and China meet. This area is the most prolific grower of the poppy seed that becomes opium and feeds the opium traffic!

On another visit to Asia during this period, I was invited by my friend Dr. J. Christy Wilson, a Christian "tentmaker" in Kabul, Afghanistan, to be present and to give the message at the dedication of the first ever Christian church in the Afghanistan capital. Christy and his Christian colleagues who were serving as medical people, teachers, etc. in the country had formed a strong congregation of expatriates who built a beautiful blue-roofed church on the outskirts of the city. The Sunday morning of the dedication ceremony there were hundreds of diplomats and other expatriates who attended the service in the midst of this strong Muslim situation. Dorothy was with me for that period of time and we were special guests of the Wilsons in their Kabul home.

It was some years later that the Muslim leadership was tremendously irritated by the strong presence of this Christian witness and destroyed this lovely church. However, the witness continued with a strong house church movement with many Muslims secretly coming to faith in Christ.

On one particular visit to London, I attended the morning service at the famed Westminster Chapel, pastored by the noted Dr. Martin Lloyd-Jones. I had heard that the pastor, in his morning pastoral prayer, would pray for as long as fifteen minutes, almost as long as his sermons. This prayer seemed to be the highlight of every Sunday morning worship service. I did time the prayer the morning I was there and it was indeed fifteen minutes in length!

Following the service, along with a World Vision colleague, I visited with Dr. Lloyd-Jones in his study. I expected to have a warm response from him but it was not to be. When he learned that I was part of a parachurch ministry he began to decry that fact and, in his comments, mentioned his disagreement with Billy Graham in his evangelistic altar calls. Though he had some strong feelings and even misgivings concerning certain large Christian organizations, I did recognize that this famed minister had a powerful influence all across Great Britain and was certainly one of the pre-eminent Bible teachers of our day.

Early on during this decade my colleague Ed Dayton and I sensed a need for training in the arena of personal and corporate time management with pastors and Christian leaders. Thus, over time we developed a two-day seminar which we called Managing Your Time. We promoted this seminar through various World Vision channels and in Christian publications and it proved to be an immediate success. Over a period of ten or twelve years we conducted literally scores of seminars in major cities across the country with an average attendance of over 150 leaders. We developed a working manual which seemed to prove helpful to all the attendees. Oftentimes those who attended one seminar came back two and sometimes three times later. We conducted these seminars, with a charge of $125 per individual, in practically every major city across the country.

In time, we also were invited to lead these seminars in a number of cities in Africa, India, Hong Kong, Brazil, Japan, the Philippines and in Canada. It was a most enjoyable experience for me to work closely with my brilliant colleague Ed Dayton and to form friendships with hundreds of leaders as a result of the seminars across the world.

It was gratifying to note the growing interest in practical time management in other cultures besides the West. The seminars were well received by Third World Christian workers and leaders who shared with us in these various overseas assignments.

To accompany the Managing Your Time seminars, we began to write and distribute the "Christian Leadership Letter." This was a four-page Kiplinger style letter that was offered free to any who asked for it. The circulation began with just a few hundred copies distributed and after almost ten years of its being published, reached a total of more than 20,000 leaders across the nation. The letters in turn evolved into two books which Ed and I co-authored entitled *The 60-Second Management Guide* and the best-selling *Strategy for Living*.

I first met the guru of the world of management, Dr. Peter

Drucker, early in 1970. One day, while visiting with my physician in his office, he mentioned that he was Peter Drucker's family doctor. I told my doctor friend that I was keenly interested in Dr. Drucker and read practically everything that he had written.

My friend said, "Would you like to meet Drucker?" "Indeed, I would," I responded.

It was then that my friend invited Dr. and Mrs. Drucker and Dorothy and me to a dinner occasion at his home. Dorothy was ill that evening and so my daughter JoAnn became my dinner partner.

It was a fascinating experience to meet with this internationally known author, teacher and management expert. He is a marvelous raconteur and a man of great wisdom. Born in Austria, trained in Germany and England, he learned Danish in order to teach Kierkegaard in Copenhagen! In the 1930s he came to America and in the ensuing years became a consultant to many of the largest corporations in the country.

In subsequent years, my friendship with this gentleman developed through various conferences I attended where he spoke and at other times when I was privileged to share in fellowship with him. Dr. Drucker was strongly spiritually influenced by friends like Dr. David Hubbard, president of Fuller Seminary, and Mr. Max DePree, chairman of the board of Herman Miller Furniture, a Fortune 500 company.

During the first part of the 1970s I had the privilege to become well acquainted with a very special African-American friend, John Perkins. Over the years John has made a tremendous impact upon the American church in the area of racial reconciliation. It was during this period that John invited me to visit him and his work and ministry in Mendenhall, Mississippi, where he had been brutally attacked by police officers and jailed because of his color and his stand on reconciliation.

My visit was just a few years after that experience, when he had opened a health clinic in this small Mississippi town. This program had captured the imagination of many people across the nation, and World Vision was privileged to be one of its many early supporters. A bit later John invited me to conduct a management seminar for black leaders at Jackson State University in Jackson, Mississippi.

My relationship with John has been a very special one which I have valued and appreciated over all of these years. Without question, he is one of the key black leaders in our evangelical world during these past decades.

Significant contributions to the decade included my friend Ken Taylor's completion of the widely selling *Living Bible*, Hal Lindsey's previously-mentioned book, *The Late Great Planet Earth*, which sold in the millions, and the developing of the Teen Challenge program under the guidance of David Wilkerson, bringing addicted teenagers to Christ.

During this decade of the 70s I was asked by the members of the annual Easter Sunrise service held at the famed Pasadena Rose Bowl to serve as chairman of these sunrise services on four early Easter mornings. I invited four special friends to be the speakers on these occasions, including author Keith Miller, Dan Liu, the beautiful committed Christian police chief from Honolulu, theologian Dr. Carl F.H. Henry, and Illinois Congressman John Anderson, who later was a candidate on the Independent ticket for the U.S. presidency. Each of these men brought a strong Resurrection message and the services were well attended with 7,000 or 8,000 people who came to that famed site at 5:30 on Easter Sunday morning. The Lord blessed with wonderfully clear weather for each of the services.

In an interesting contrast, a bit later in the decade I was invited to bring the message on Easter Sunday morning at the Riverside, California, service held on top of Mount Rubidoux. It was an outdoor service and we were drenched with heavy rain which never ceased! An expected crowd of several thousand amounted to only 100 or so brave souls!

In this decade I was honored to have formed a warm friendship with Dr. David Hubbard, president of Fuller Theological Seminary. I was privileged to serve on several ad hoc committees and boards related to the seminary and was invited on occasion, as well, to teach classes on evangelism, management principles and leadership.

Dr. Hubbard and I shared a deep concern for the training of lay leadership and on two occasions invited 75 to 100 key lay leaders to share in two-day conferences in what we called Leadership Dialogues. We agreed on the guest list and found it to be a most rewarding experience. One of these conferences was held at a hotel in Palm Springs, California, and the second one in Santa Barbara, with a different group of laity in each of the two meaningful two-day seminars.

Early in this decade a "heads up" alert came from Senator Mark Hatfield's office in Washington that nonprofit organizations were going to be more carefully monitored by government agencies, particularly related to fund–raising activities. If we as evangelical nonprofit ministries were not able to monitor ourselves there would be significant legislation introduced which could be hurtful to many ministries.

Following a high level meeting with the Senator in his office in Washington, our leadership in World Vision and the Billy Graham Evangelistic Association determined to give guidance and direction to the formation of an association to set up standards which would be self-regulating. The determination to do this seemed to satisfy those in Washington who were threatening to present the legislation, and thus George Wilson of the BGEA, Stan Mooneyham, and I convened a group of twenty-five or thirty leaders from sister organizations to discuss this challenge. As a result came the formation of the ECFA (Evangelical Council for Financial Accountability) and I was asked to serve as its first chairman of the board.

Immediately there was high interest in joining this association with several score of agency leaders who became charter members. Over the years since that time there have been almost

1,000 evangelical agencies who have aligned themselves with the ECFA, which presently plays a significant role from its offices in the nation's capital. Several directors have led the organization including Olan Hendrix, Arthur Borden and presently Paul Nelson.

Senator Hatfield became a special friend during these days. I had the privilege of visiting with him on numerous occasions in his lovely Washington Senate Office Building office, as well as being a guest in his homes, both in Georgetown and Newport, Oregon. Mark was always so responsive in helping us resolve problems related to visas or special government contacts. During this time he served for a period of several years as a member of our World Vision board of directors. He always proved to be a godly, spiritual counselor and a strong representative of our faith in the nation's capital—as well as in his previous assignments as Secretary of State and Governor of Oregon.

One of the key evangelists of our day, who began his ministry in this period of time, is Luis Palau, an Argentinian who graduated from Multnomah Bible College (formerly Multnomah School of the Bible) in Portland, Oregon. Luis and I formed a friendship early on in his ministry while he was associated as an evangelist with Overseas Crusades.

When he left OC during the 70s he asked if I would serve on the board of directors as his new ministry of international evangelism was launched. I was happy to do so and for a number of years met with Luis and colleagues on the board of this significant evangelistic ministry which has reached across every continent and which God has so wonderfully and richly blessed over these years. Luis has remained a very special friend from the day we first met.

It was in this decade that Bible reading increased as new translations of the Scriptures abounded. Ken Taylor finished the paraphrased Living Bible, and Roman Catholics released their first ecumenical edition of the Scriptures to be granted from Rome. The New American Standard Bible, developed by the Lockman Foundation, was also released through a group of publishers including Regal Books and Creation House, and the Gideon Bible reached a circulation of one hundred million!

The Christian Management Association (originally known as The Christian Ministries Management Association) began in this period, initially under the leadership of Sylvia Nash and later John Pearson. It was my privilege to serve as chairman of the board of this fine association for a number of years. It began with a couple dozen ministries involved and presently has over 800 members. The training in Christian management for Christian nonprofit agencies has made a significant impact upon those who have shared in the association.

I was invited by a Christian travel agency to go with my friend Dr. Harold Lindsell on a Greek Island cruise for ten days. We had about 90 Christian passengers on this Greek ship in the Mediterranean and day by day Harold and I shared in the lectures—he speaking of the Seven Churches of the Revelation, and I speaking of the journeys of the Apostle Paul—as we visited such places as Ephesus and Philippi. Dorothy and I thoroughly enjoyed and appreciated this special relaxing opportunity. A highlight for me was a visit to the island of Patmos. We visited the cave where purportedly 2,000 years ago the Apostle John was given and wrote the apocalyptic vision—the book of Revelation.

The tradition of the early church was that John was banished to the island in the reign of Domitian, sometime between A.D. 94 and A.D. 96. Patmos is a barren, rockly little island approximately forty miles off the coast of Turkey. The Romans often banished political prisoners to such remote islands. Such banishment involved the loss of civil rights and of all property except enough money to take care of a bare existence. It was here that the Apostle received that magnificent Word from the Lord.

I was deeply appreciative of receiving a couple of special recognition awards during this decade, including the Distinguished Service Award from Messiah College, where I gave the commencement address, and the International Leadership Award from the International School of Theology in Arrowhead Springs, California. Also, my colleagues at Taylor University named me the Alumnus of the Year for that school and, some years later, I was given what is known as the Legion of Honor Award. It was during this time as well that the National Religious Broadcasters, at their annual Convention in Washington, D.C., presented me with what they call their Distinguished Service Award. Undeserved—but deeply appreciated!

Earlier on in this book I mentioned the formation of the National Association of Evangelicals. In its earliest years I attended almost all of the association's conventions held annually across the nation. At the 1970 convention, held in Denver, I was honored by receiving the NAE Layman of the Year Award. My old friend Bob Cook was president of the NAE at that time and he very fittingly made the presentation which was so deeply appreciated. The plaque still hangs on my study wall.

Some of the Christian personalities who made a decided impact on me and my responsibilities in this decade included authors Francis Schaeffer, J.I. Packer, Bernard Ramm, Malcolm Muggeridge and Charles Colson. Other key personalities who were friends of mine making an impact during these years included Ron Sider, then professor at Messiah College and author of *Rich Christians in an Age of Hunger*, Vernon Grounds, president of the Conservative Baptist Seminary in Denver; Graham Kerr , the "Galloping Gourmet," who came to Christ at this time; Joni Eareckson (later Tada), quadriplegic speaker and author of the best-selling book, *Joni*; Dr. Bob Schuller of the Crystal Cathedral in Southern California; and Jim Wallace of *Sojourners* magazine.

Beginning with my years in book publishing with the Zondervan Publishing House, I have had a continuing high level of interest in Christian book publication. Along the way I worked closely with my friend Bob Van Kampen with the Van Kampen Press, headquartered in Wheaton, Illinois. And with another friend, Al Smith, we formed for a short period of time a small book publishing firm which we called Miracle Books. Al funded the business and asked me to serve as president of that organization, which I did for a period of time during this decade. It was later in the 70s that my friend Sam Moore, president of Thomas Nelson Publishers in Nashville, approached me about the possibility of my leaving World Vision and becoming president of Nelson organization. Though I felt the Lord led me to decline Sam's kind offer, I have had an identification with both Word Books, as a member of the initial advisory board with my friend, company president Jarrell McCracken, and also served as chairman of the board of Here's Life Publishers, a division of Campus Crusade for Christ. (Once getting printer's ink in one's veins, it's difficult to stay away from the world of publishing.)

During these days I found myself deeply involved in writing in the arena of Christian leadership and management. I was able to write—or co-author on occasion—quite a number of books published by some of my publisher friends at Zondervan, Word Books, Regal Publications, Fleming Revell and Thomas Nelson. Some of these titles included *The Making of a Christian Leader* (which became for Zondervan a best-seller), *Integrity, The Fine Art of Friendship, Managing Your Time* (also a best-seller), *The Pursuit of Excellence, Strategy for Living, Your Gift of Administration, Motivation to Last a Lifetime* and a few others.

Following many years of leadership in the 50s and 60s in Youth for Christ, many of us who shared in the ministry moved into other areas of outreach. A few of us who worked closely together felt it might be meaningful if we could meet annually someplace across the nation for a weekend of fellowship, prayer and sharing of God's working in our lives.

Thus, seven couples from the YFC leadership determined to form what we called a "YFC Old Guard." These included Dave and Carol Breese, Jack and Carol Sonneveldt, Wendy and Norma Collins, Roy and Marianne McKeown, Jack and Marijean Hamilton, Evon and Jean Hedley and Dorothy and me. Beginning in early 1970 we met annually someplace across the country for the reunion weekend. It proved to be a tremendously encouraging time together as we convened in places like Hilton Head, South Carolina, at Monterey in northern California, in Phoenix, Kansas City, Chicago, Palm Springs and many other places.

As we met together we would share God's leading in our lives, pray for our families, rejoice in God's goodness and simply enjoy each other. These "Old Guard" conclaves continue to this day.

——— ——— ———

The 1970s was, indeed, a decade of "Disillusionment."
As a result, we witnessed both the "ying" and the "yang!"

"Nationally in this decade there was a host of significant highlights. Among them was the shooting of popular President Ronald Reagan by John Hinckley, Jr., the appointment of Sandra Day O'Connor to be the first woman Supreme Court Justice, and Geraldine Ferraro being named as the Democratic vice presidential candidate running with Senator Walter Mondale. Four Reagan-Gorbachev summits were conducted and the space shuttle Columbia was launched for the first time, followed later by the **Challenger** *tragedy."*

5

REFLECTIONS

The 1980s — A Decade of Unrest

THE DECADE OF THE 1980S WAS MARKED BY A GREAT deal of unrest and unease, both nationally and internationally, in the economic, political, social and spiritual arenas. Change cascaded upon us with our cyber-society and the use of computer technology—the introduction of facsimile machines, the earliest version of the Internet and all the enhancements which our computerized society had to wrestle with. We seemed torn between a call to greatness in our national and personal lives, the temptation to greed and selfishness in a land of opportunity, and a nostalgic longing for a time of certainty, stability and calm.

Nationally in this decade there was a host of significant highlights. Among them was the shooting of popular President Ronald Reagan by John Hinckley, Jr., the appointment of Sandra Day O'Connor to be the first woman Supreme Court Justice, and Geraldine Ferraro being named as the Democratic vice presidential candidate running with Senator Walter Mondale. Four Reagan-Gorbachev summits were conducted and the space shuttle *Columbia* was launched for the first time, followed later by the *Challenger* tragedy.

In 1981 Anwar Sadat in Egypt was assassinated. One year later, AIDS was first discovered. Prime Minister Indira Gandhi, whom, with Bob Pierce I had once met, was murdered in 1984. In 1982 Israel invaded Lebanon, and then withdrew in 1985.

The Soviet Union had a most troublesome five year period from 1980-1985. Brezhnev was their leader in 1982, Andropov in 1984 and Chernenko in 1985. All dissidents in the USSR were treated harshly, a protracted war in Afghanistan drained the country of human and material resources, and immigration was restricted.

Late in the decade we saw the dramatic failure of Marxist economics in Hungary, East Germany, Czechoslovakia, Bulgaria and Romania. At the very end of the period the entire world seemed to watch as the infamous Berlin Wall fell and East Germany was opened to the world.

In June of 1989 an estimated 5,000 to 7,000 students and workers were mercilessly killed in the Tienanmen Square massacre in Beijing, China. As a result, martial law was imposed. Increasingly across the world there was both sinister threats and actual acts of terrorism.

The European community was becoming a Common Market of over 300 million people, changing the landscape of Europe forever. On a brighter, more romantic note, in July of 1981 there was the worldwide viewing of the wedding of Prince Charles (the future King of England) to Lady Diana Spencer in St. Paul's Cathedral in London. Three-fourths of the world was able to witness this event immediately as it occurred by means of international television.

The decade also marked a major and unprecedented spiritual revival—together with spiritual hunger—in much of Africa, Asia and Latin America, most particularly in Argentina following the Falkland Islands crisis in 1982.

Futurologist Tom Sine gave us, early in the decade, "an agenda for the 1980s." His list included global hunger, euthanasia and dying with dignity, genetic engineering, nuclear holocaust, technology and dimished privacy, a polarized society and church renewal. All of these predicted items made their impact upon society in this decade.

One observer, writing of the changing Christian scene of this decade, stated: "We have a second generation of leadership that acknowledges valid differences among Christian entities but, at the same time, realizes that the issues are bigger than each group can handle singly." Many Christian organizations began to work together on such common problems as personnel management, increased government reporting requirements, and the growing tendency to file lawsuits. It was noted as well that almost all leaders of the parachurch groups believed there was a growing degree of professionalism within their organizations. Evangelists and youth workers went to management seminars, and evangelical boards hired trained managers, marketing directors and public relations experts.

The decade also marked the growth of a host of various parachurch ministries, focusing on prison ministries, ethnic groups, and simple lifestyle, through organizations such as Prison Fellowship, the Sojourners, Jews for Jesus, Evangelicals for Social Action and the Christian Broadcasting Network (CBN). In addition, over 100 new overseas mission agencies were founded in the U.S. in the 80s.

The American populus had a growing awareness of the severe problem of homelessness all across the nation amidst our affluence, with a realization that children comprised forty percent of all U.S. poor. In addition twenty million U.S. children were living with a single or step-parent.

The decades-old East African revival movement continued on, outpacing some of the highest population growth in the world. Alongside this, in Africa there was rapid economic decline in most nations, together with desertification, world economic recession which hit the continent very hard, heavy indebtedness, a large population increase, and great political instability, together with the tragic Ethiopia famine affecting 150 million Africans.

This decade marked the increasing awareness of the rapid growth of the charismatic movement, not only in Third World nations but most particularly in North America. There were an estimated 300 million of these believers worldwide in 1988. Pollster George Gallup found in 1980 that nineteen percent of all Americans considered themselves to be charismatic Christians.

Part of the spiritual vitality experienced in the U.S. was expressed in July of 1980 through the American Festival of Evangelism in Kansas City, focusing on the unreached peoples of America. It was my personal privilege to work with my friend general superintendent Tom Zimmerman of the Assemblies of God as chairman, and I as secretary, of the sponsoring committee. The impact of this convocation was felt across the nation as groups of churches and Christians united in prayer and action to lovingly communicate the Gospel message where it had not been received.

The 1980s also marked the amazing growth of the electronic church with an estimated 130 million viewers every week. Focusing on world evangelization, there was a thirty-three percent increase of career U.S. missionaries in this decade, plus the phenomenal 30,000 additional short-term personnel from the U.S. sent through 250 different evangelical agencies. A growing international phenomena also was occurring during this period, resulting in an estimated 15,000 Third World missionaries representing 400 societies, from Asia, Africa and Latin America.

———   ———   ———

During this period we saw the passing of many founder/ visionaries who, prior to their deaths, placed leadership on others who were not around at the beginning of the ministry. As a result, many original supporters were gone. A constituency now existed that knew little of the early glory days, but were asked to stand behind the pioneering work. The challenge was to cultivate entire new constituencies for the important next generation of these ministries. The decade also marked a significant increase in the leadership of women in our evangelical world, both in the church and parachurch movements. In addition, there developed women's Bible study luncheons and fellowship groups,

Winning Women, Women Aglow, and Women Alive, as well as strengthening of the older Christian Women's Clubs which were more traditional. Much of the world publicly witnessed the tragic moral failures of Christian leaders such as Jimmy Bakker, founder of the national Praise The Lord telecast and Jimmy Swaggart, charismatic televangelist.

Although early in the PTL ministry I was a guest on the program with Jim and Tammy Faye Bakker, Dorothy and I were uncomfortable visiting the dramatic, posh headquarters of the ministry in South Carolina, with all of its glitz and glitter, and felt we would have to decline further invitations.

Early in this decade my friend and colleague Stan Mooneyham, following a time of separation from his wife La Verda and their impending divorce, was asked to resign from the presidency of World Vision—which he did, reluctantly. I was requested by our World Vision board to take over the reins as president, a challenge I accepted with a great deal of fear and trepidation! However, it has been a most rewarding experience for me, one which I have thoroughly enjoyed and appreciated. Presiding over a giant organization like World Vision, quite possibly the largest NGO (Non-governmental Organization), was a humbling experience. I have been so grateful for the strong staff that had been formed for the World Vision ministry in the U.S. and leaned heavily on these wonderful colleagues in providing leadership for the ever-expanding WV ministry into almost 100 nations across the world.

All of my life I have had a keen interest in China. As a boy in a missionary-minded home, I recall my parents often had missionaries visit with us, many of whom had been or were missionaries in that country. As well, early on in my work with the Zondervan Publishing House, I wrote several brief missionary biographies of those who had ministered in China, including the famed founder of the China Inland Mission, J. Hudson Taylor, and Robert Morrison. Thus, when the doors began to creep open again for visitors to go to The People's Republic, I arranged, in 1981, for Dorothy and me to join a tour group from Hong Kong going into that nation just recovering from the years of Communist oppression. Our group visited several cities, including Beijing, Nanking, Shanghai, and other points of interest.

One Sunday morning during that trip, Dorothy and I left the tour group who were going to the Great Wall and found our way by means of a taxi to one of only two Protestant churches open at that time in the city of Beijing. It was not a large church, but it was packed to the doors with Chinese Christians quietly worshipping together. There were perhaps fifteen or twenty Bibles on a table in the rear of the church, which were passed along by members of the congregation to be able to be read during the service, for obviously they did not have access to Bibles at that time. We seemed to be the only foreigners there, but we were warmly welcomed by the members of the congregation and were invited to tea with them following the service.

It was almost impossible to hire a taxi in that part of the city so it was suggested that we ask our taxi driver to remain until after the service was over, and then take us back to the Forbidden City where we were scheduled to meet our tour group as they returned from the Great Wall. Amazingly, amidst a crowd of literally tens of thousands of people in the Square, our taxi and the tour bus met at the entrance of the Forbidden City and we were able to rejoin our group.

My friend Jonathan Chao's wife, from Hong Kong, arranged to meet us in Shanghai during our last two or three days in China. Jonathan is a key "China watcher" and a key analyst of the church movement in China. Jonathan arranged for his wife to escort us to a couple of the churches in Shanghai. One which we visited was the Methodist Church where the old pastor told us that World Vision founder Bob Pierce had preached in the late 1940s! It had been a warehouse during the revolution and had just reopened.

As we were going through customs and immigration to leave Shanghai to return to Hong Kong, we were held up for more than an hour by the authorities who wanted to know why we were in China, what we were taking out of the country, and why we were with this particular lady from Hong Kong. After carefully examining each piece of our luggage, they finally and reluctantly let us through in order to rejoin the group to fly back to Hong Kong.

——— ——— ———

During this time I served as chairman of the English Language Institute for China (ELIC) board. My friend Ken Wendling, the president of the ministry, had invited me on two different occasions to see the work of our ELIC teachers in China. The first of these visits included time with our teachers in Xian, city of the famed Terra Cotta soldiers and horses that had been excavated just a few decades previously. Incidentally, in Xian we stayed in a new hotel just built by my friend Winston Ko, from Southern California.

We traveled on to west China to the city of Chengdu. Terry Madison, editor of our *World Vision* magazine and a friend of ELIC, was with Ken and me late one night when we hired two bicycle rickshaws to travel across the city to view it. I recalled that Chengdu was the city where martyred missionaries John and Betty Stam had been cruelly murdered many years prior to our visit. I had written the biography of these two wonderful Reformed Church missionaries, and I wanted to see and sense something of where they were when they were martyred.

We then flew up to Tibet to the capital city of Lhasa, at 12,000 feet, which is the highest capital in the world. It was necessary for us to use oxygen on occasion because of the shortness of breath at that high altitude. We visited with government authorities regarding placing teachers of English in the university and were warmly welcomed by the Tibetan leadership. It was such a fascinating experience to be in that isolated nation where there were only a handful of foreigners and a minimal number of secret believers.

An American, Robert Morse, a member of a famed missionary family who ministered for years in Burma, was spending time teaching at the university in Lhasa. He heard we were in the city and came to visit us at the small hotel where we lodged. He gave us great encouragement regarding the planned program for Tibet where, since that time, ELIC has sent a number of Christian teachers, particularly from Canada, since U.S. citizens have had great difficulty in gaining entry into Tibet. Tibet is ninety-nine percent a Buddhist nation under the exiled Dalai Lama, presently living in India. We visited the giant Buddhist monastery on the outskirts of the city with its 999 rooms!

On a later visit with Ken Wendling to China, I went with special ELIC donor friends, who were invited by the ministry to observe the work of the teachers in numbers of the cities where they were teaching English to university students. Gratefully, Dorothy was able to join with me on this particular visit and to meet with these key Christian teachers who were living so sacrificially in order to minister in the name of Christ.

My travels during this busy decade took me to many incredible places where I saw the Gospel being proclaimed. Following are some of the places and experiences that touched me most profoundly:

Africa

On numerous occasions during the decade of the 80s, I visited the struggling African nation of Ethiopia, which was experiencing its worst famine in history. Sometimes I would take World Vision donors along to observe the work we were carrying on to alleviate this terrible time of suffering and starvation in that nation with a history going back more than two millenia.

A highlight was what was known as the "Ansokia Project" in which we in World Vision helped the farmers irrigate their land, plant thousands of trees, and supplied them with oxen for plowing. Our staff also gave guidance and direction to a rural development program, which eventually became an exemplary model for all of the nation.

On one trip, accompanied by our board member Herb Hawkins and his wife Betty and a few other friends, we met with the minister for agriculture to discuss with him some of the projects being conducted in Ethiopia. The minister was most gracious in affirming the work we were seeking to do as a Christian ministry to his suffering people.

At approximately the same time, I shared in a visit to the southern Sudan, which also was suffering severely from crop failures and literal starvation. Our team flew down from the capital, Khartoum, to a military site in the south where, in the midst of a strong Muslim nation, there was a wonderful band of Christian believers. It was a great joy to encourage them and to, at least in a small sense, identify with their struggles and needs. We were able to supply them with some plane loads of relief goods, medicines and other life necessities, for which they were most grateful.

On another occasion my beloved friends Steve and Iris Lazarian and our pastor, Paul Cedar accompanied me on a visit to Kenya and Zimbabwe. Steve, a gifted engineer and entrepreneur, saw a situation on one of our World Vision projects in Zimbabwe which he felt could be readily corrected, and he offered his expertise to the people who were heading up the project. Steve supplied, upon his return home, the necessary equipment which greatly enhanced the value of that particular agricultural project.

One of the highlights on a subsequent trip to Africa was a visit to Timbuktu in northern Mali, West Africa. Several supporters of World Vision were with me, along with my associate, John Foulkes, as we visited this ancient city. (Yes, there is a Timbuktu!) When we looked out the door of our humble guest house early in the morning we would see the Tuareg tribesmen with their camels out in the Sahara Desert which surrounded the little city with a population of perhaps 50,000 individuals.

The remarkable thing about this particular visit was my introduction to the only Christian pastor in the town, a man by the name of Pastor Nauk. We had heard about Nauk's ministry and arranged to visit him in his humble little shack, along with his wife and three children—surrounded in the courtyard by chickens and pigs.

Pastor Nauk told us how that as a little boy he heard about a missionary visiting his city of Timbuktu who offered a Bic pen to any children who would attend his children's meetings every morning for a week. Little Nauk had never had such a pen and because of that enticement, he attended the class each morning to earn his pen. As a result of seeing Christ's love and hearing of His salvation, at the age of nine or ten he became a believer in Christ and determined to follow Jesus.

Later the same missionary enabled Nauk to go to Bamako, the capital of Mali, to train for the ministry at a small Bible college in order to become a pastor. Following his graduation he returned to Timbuktu and began to invite neighbors in to hear the Gospel. Ultimately a church was formed. When we were there, it was the only church in town. The fifty or sixty believers met together on a weekly basis under Pastor Nauk's leadership.

Nauk told us of his burden to reach the Tuareg tribes–people who wandered the desert in that part of Mali. He said that he would often walk for days through the hot and burning sands to meet with them. When he mentioned that he walked to minister to them, I asked him if he had any transportation. He responded that he did not.

I asked a rather foolish question at that point, questioning him whether a bicycle would be of help. Laughingly he responded, "Have you ever tried to ride a bicycle in the desert?" I then asked him what we could do to be of help to him in this particular ministry. He indicated that if he had a donkey or a mule to ride in the desert it would be most advantageous. I asked him how much one would cost and he indicated about $30. Immediately our little group gave him the money and said, "Please go and buy such an animal."

Two days later he visited us at our guest house and shared that he had purchased an animal, and was simply delighted to have it to expedite his ministry among the tribes–people. This gentleman was one of the most delightful individuals I had ever met anywhere in the world.

It was on this same trip to northern Mali that our twin engine MAF Twin Otter plane flew us out about 200 kilometers east of the city. We knew that some of our World Vision people had done some pioneering work in this little village which we wanted to visit. We were warmly greeted on the dirt airstrip at the edge of town by our WV colleagues. Following a bit of lunch and a cool drink they said they had a special surprise for us.

They took us in their minivan out to the edge of town where there was an orphanage housing about forty little boys and girls who had been abandoned. Across the front of the orphanage compound was a banner which read, "The Ted Engstrom World Vision Orphanage." I was completely taken by surprise and delighted to have my name associated with such a project in that distant corner of the globe. To my knowledge, this orphanage still exists.

On another of my frequent visits to Africa, this time to the west African country of Senegal, I had the pleasure of having Russ and Cathie Reid along with me. In addition to Senegal we visited the west African nations of Burkina Faso and Mauritania. One day, while in Dakar, the Senegalese capital, we took a tour boat out to Goree, the little island from which the slave shipments were made during the early part of the nineteenth century. While there we visited what is infamously known as the "Door of No Return."

Upon coming back to the capital the little boat docked in some rocky waters, alongside a frail wharf. Seeking to disembark onto the pier, my war-damaged leg began to give way and I almost fell between the boat and the dock into the murky waters. If my former secretary, Denise Schubert, who was then on the staff of World Vision in Senegal, and an African gentleman had not grabbed me at that moment, this book would never have been written!

It was also on this visit that we were in Ooagadugo, Burkino Faso, the capital of what formerly was Upper Volta. We visited a special World Vision project some miles out from the city on a Sunday morning. I was invited to preach in the little thatched roof church stuck away in the midst of miles of tall elephant grass on a small clearing which the believers had made. We had visited a dam earlier that morning, which World Vision had paid for and sponsored. The dam provided much-needed water for the crops of the farmers in that whole area. As a result of that act of mercy, the people began to inquire why this was done on their behalf. Upon learning that it was provided by Christian friends across the world, over the ensuing months many came to faith in Christ and a church congregation was formed.

Something happened in that Sunday morning service that I had never experienced before. Following my message, translated into both the tribal language and French, I was asked by the wonderful African pastor if I would offer a prayer for the sick. I don't have the gift of healing and was reluctant to do so, but did so upon his persuasion. A score or more people came forward at the close of the service to be annointed and prayed for. I did lead in a prayer for healing for these beautifully committed new Christians who sought God's healing. It became a remarkable experience for me, never to be forgotten. It seemed like Heaven came down into that little thatched roof church as we fellowshipped with these beautiful new believers.

Later that evening, in the midst of this very poor and dirty capital city of Ooagadugo, we were invited by some lovely Roman Catholic nuns to have supper in their pleasant retreat center. It was an amazing oasis in the midst of that primitive community where we were served a lovely supper and listened to these French nuns sing Ave Maria as we enjoyed their hospitality.

One of the outstanding ministries in Eastern Africa today is Daystar Christian University, located in Nairobi, Kenya. It was founded early in the 80s by some concerned national leaders and missionaries as they brought into being this Christian university, under the guidance and direction of its president, my friend Stephen Talitwala.

I had the privilege of serving on the U.S. support board for this fine institution, visited it on several occasions and gave lectures to the fine African student body. The college has had remarkable growth and has exerted an evangelical influence all across the continent. It was most gratifying to be a part of the early days of this significant institution. It is supported in its degree program by both Messiah College in Pennsylvania and Wheaton College in Illinois. Stephen Talitwala has served these years as its principal (or in American terms, its president).

Cambodia

During the Cambodian crisis, and just prior to the fall of the capital, Phnom Penh, World Vision chartered an aircraft to fly several score of Cambodian babies and their caretakers out of the city and ultimately to be flown to the United States. I met the contingent of these babies and helpers at the Travis Air Force Base in northern California and helped to arrange for their care at a hospital facility in the Bay Area. A few days later I accompanied a group of twenty or more of these infants to Southern California where, after a period of time, all were adopted into Christian homes. We have lost track of many of these children, but we have been able to keep in touch with many others over the years. Some have gone on to college and have other responsibilities.

In the midst of the Cambodian crisis, President Jimmy Carter invited several of us who headed NGOs (Nonprofit Governmental Organizations) working in that nation to meet with him at the White House. We met in the Cabinet Room with the President and two or three of his staff members, as well as representatives from the State Department. The President was most gracious and listened carefully to our concerns relative to the military involvement and societal problems of Cambodia. I was privileged to share in this discussion with my colleagues in sister organizations, some evangelical and some secular, as well as with some of our church leaders, including the Archbishop of the Boston Diocese of the Roman Catholic Church.

We sat around the large Cabinet Room table and I was honored to sit just two seats away from the President, on his right. He greeted each of us personally and warmly and expressed deep appreci-ation for our involvement in that crisis area of the world during that period of time.

Poland

One of the key nations in Eastern Europe where World Vision has had a ministry for many years is Poland. Our World Vision director for that part of the world, Ralph Hamburger, invited then WV board chairman, Gordon MacDonald, and me to spend a week visiting our various projects in a nation that then was behind the Iron Curtain. It was a great joy to meet simple, sincere

Christians who had struggled so deeply following the days of World War II.

World Vision had supplied large containers of food, material, clothing and other necessities, which were distributed by the wonderful, but struggling evangelical church in that nation. Gordon, Ralph and I were invited to have tea (as well as vodka, which we politely refused) with the Metropolitan of the Roman Catholic Church. He was most gracious in his comments concerning the work and ministry of World Vision in behalf of suffering people, and particularly with the entire Church in that nation.

One of the highlights of that trip was a visit to the birth-place and home of the famed musician, Frederick Chopin. As we walked through the delightful gardens and into the cottage where he lived, we constantly heard the strains of Chopin music in an utterly delightful setting.

Egypt

Sharing with Sam Kamaleson and other members of a World Vision Ministers Conference team, we led a most rewarding five-day-long conference in Alexandria, Egypt, attended primarily by the ancient Coptic church leaders, together with some of the few evangelical leaders in that nation. Our Coptic friends were most appreciative of our presentations and warmly welcomed us into their fellowship. It was during the same visit to Egypt that I was able to view the famed Pyramids and the Sphinx, near Cairo, which are absolute architectural miracles dating back several millenia.

On one of my frequent visits to Europe during this time, I spent one day in meeting with some of the leadership of the World Council of Churches in Geneva and later the same day visited the World Health Organization headquarters as well as the headquarters of the International Red Cross. In each of these situations I was well received and was able to share something of our burden and vision in the ministries God has given us in World Vision. Our more theologically liberal brothers at the

World Council were most gracious as we shared our luncheon time together.

Korea

One of the projects sponsored by World Vision in Korea was the organizing of what is known as ACTS (The Asia Center for Theological Studies). Through the efforts of Marlin Nelson and others of our World Vision personnel resident in Seoul, this graduate theological seminary was begun on the World Vision hospitality property. I was asked to serve on the board of the seminary, with some of our Korean friends, and we invited a special friend of mine, Dr. Han Chul Ha, to become our president.

Over the years this seminary has grown in influence and impact, training graduate students not only from across Korea, but from many other countries in Asia. Later a U.S. support board was formed with Marlin Nelson, who became a professor at ACTS, as our secretary/treasurer and I was asked to serve as the chairperson. Over these years several hundred choice young men and women have been trained theologically and are actively serving the Lord all across South Korea in churches and missions—as well as else-where in Asia such as the Philippines, Bangladesh, India, Burma and Pakistan.

Co-Laboring With Christian Leaders

I have had a long-standing concern for and interest in sharing with fellow leaders in the evangelical community. Early in the 80s I sensed that leaders in this community were hungry for fellowship beyond their own environs and thus I decided to sponsor what I called the "CEO Dialogues."

I began to invite select leaders to meet together for a day simply to share experiences, burdens and challenges in the work. Over the course of a dozen years or so I was able to bring groups of twenty-five or thrity leaders to spend a day in a hotel in some city across the nation. In these thirty or forty different sessions we met in cities from New York City to San Diego and from Seattle to Dallas. My associate, John Foulkes, helped in organizing these dialogues which seemingly proved to be eminently worthwhile and profitable.

We would meet from 9 a.m. until 4 p.m. and have our lunch together. Our conversations were held completely confidential and, amazingly, during these sessions oftentimes there would be times of confession, prayer for each other, sharing of heavy burdens with fellow leaders and, without exception, following the dialogue session there was a sense of the Lord having met with us as co-workers in the Kingdom, each having a different role to play in our various ministries. Later these "dialogues" were turned over to my friends in the Christian Management Association.

In 1980, I was invited by my beloved friend Dr. James Dobson to become a member of the board of Focus on the Family, then a burgeoning new radio ministry. It happened that my friend Bobb Biehl suggested that Dr. Dobson would like to have lunch with me some day and so we arranged to have a meeting with the three of us at the Pasadena University Club.

In the midst of our conversation Jim said he would be very appreciative if I would consider becoming a member of the board of his new ministry. I indicated to him that my fork was pretty full with the load I was carrying in my leadership in World Vision, plus serving on several other evangelical boards, so at the time I declined.

Jim indicated that he had completed a new video series on the family and suggested that he would be happy to have it shown to members of our WV staff. So, I invited him some weeks later to come to my office and have it projected before our senior staff. The portion of the video he showed had to do with the importance of the father figure in the home. In the midst of the film showing I sent a note to Jim in which I wrote, "Count me in!" That began a very warm friendship and involvement over the years as a board member with the Focus ministry.

Early on there were only a half dozen of us who were on the board, four of whom were staff members. (These, apart from Jim and Shirley Dobson, were later released from this responsibility so that the governing board could be primarily outsiders.) The first board meeting that I attended was in the Dobson home in Arcadia, California, with only six or eight of us present. Since that time the board has been enlarged to a dozen key members who fly in from across the country for our three-times-a-year, two-day board sessions. It has been a joy and delight to serve this significant ministry over the years, and I have missed no more than two or three regulary scheduled meetings throughout all of this time.

When I joined the Focus board the national divorce rate was up about seventy percent over the previous ten years. The average marriage was lasting only six years and more than forty percent of the children in the nation lived in one parent homes. Very courageously, Jim Dobson has addressed these family issues, as well as many other significant political issues that affect the moral values of our nation.

———   ———   ———

I have always had a high interest in Christian higher education, and have been pleased to serve on the board of trustees at Taylor University, George Fox College, Azusa Pacific University and The International School of Theology. During the 80s I had the honor and privilege of giving commencement addresses at a number of Christian colleges and universities, which has always been a personal joy and delight. The schools at which I gave the commencement address included Trinity Evangelical Seminary, Northwestern College in Minneapolis, Crown College in Minnesota, Marion College in Indiana (now Indiana Wesleyan University), St. Paul Bible College, Seattle Pacific University, John Brown University, Sterling College in Kansas and Tabor College, also in Kansas. I also delivered the commencement address at my alma mater, Taylor University. Five of these colleges and universities gave me honorary doctorates—which, as I have often said, are non-negotiable, but nevertheless deeply appreciated!

Another significant involvement during this period of time was my joining the board of the International School of Theology at the Campus Crusade for Christ headquarters in Arrowhead Springs, California. This seminary program was launched in 1980 by Dr. Bill Bright and its first president was Dr. Ron Jenson. I joined the board early on during Ron's leadership. The second president was Dr. James McHann, followed by Dr. Don Weaver. For much of this time I have had the privilege of serving as board chairman. The seminary has graduated scores of men and women who are providing strong evangelical leadership all across the world. All twelve board members have become choice and dear friends, as have the three presidents and many of the professors at the school.

Following a number of years of service on the George Fox College board, I resigned my position when my friend David Le Shana left the college to become president at Seattle Pacific University.

About that time, in 1980, Dr. Paul Sage, president of Azusa Pacific University, asked if I would be willing to serve as one of that school's directors. I agreed and have found it to be an exciting and rewarding experience. The members of this board are highly gifted and qualified men and women and it has been a pleasure to share with them in determining policy matters related to the university. I have been privileged to serve for several years as chairman of the board and on one occasion gave the commencement address.

During the days of a pastor's conference in Calcutta, India, sharing with Sam Kamaleson and Charles Blair, pastor of the large Calvary Temple in Denver, arrangements were made for Charles and me to have a visit with Mother Teresa in her Sisters of Mercy home for the indigent. This remarkable, godly Roman Catholic nun spent the better part of an hour with us discussing her work and learning what we were doing in Calcutta during that time. She was unhurried in her conversation and was genuinely interested in our visiting her and the work she founded and headed up in ministering to the destitute and dying off the streets of that Indian city. It was an unforgettable experience to meet with this winner of the Nobel Peace Prize and a woman of international acclaim and appreciation.

I have had a longstanding interest in and involvement with my friends at Fuller Seminary. I was invited by David Hubbard, the seminary president, to chair the board of the Institute of Christian Organizational Development. Sharing with me in this endeavor were Ed Dayton and David Secunda, vice president of the American Management Association. This program became an integral part of the seminary curriculum devoted to the theme of organizational development.

Dr. Donald McGavran, dean of the Fuller Seminary School of World Mission, became a special friend during these days. He and I served together on the board of the Institute of American Church Growth founded by Dr. Win Arn. What a delight it was to learn from this wise missionary statesman. A Yale-educated Ph.D., Dr. McGavran ministered for two decades among the illiterate peasants of small rural villages in India. He covered vast areas in this evangelistic work, often traveling by bicycle or on foot, having with him a team of Indian evangelists and pastors to start a "people movement" among one of the casts.

Dr. McGavran was known as the founder of the Church Growth Movement which began during this decade. I was privileged to meet often with him in various settings related to this burgeoning movement. He was the founding dean of the School of World Mission, beginning this role at age 67.

At the same time I was also privileged to share with my special friend—and McGarvan protege—Peter Wagner in many of these church growth conclaves. Peter also served as an adjunct professor at Fuller.

It was in this interesting decade that I had contact with many of our choice Christian leaders, enjoying fellowship with them under varying circumstances. Included were my mentoree, Jay

Kesler, president of Taylor University; the dynamic Joni Eareckson Tada, who started her ministry to the disabled in this period; Robert (Bob) Schuller, pastor of the Crystal Cathedral in Garden Grove, California; John MacArthur, Jr., pastor of the large Grace Community Church in the Los Angeles area; Stuart and Jill Briscoe, pastors of the Elmbrook Bible Church in Wisconsis; Richard Foster, the author of the best-seller *Celebration of Discipline*; Charles Colson, founder of the Prison Fellowship and President Nixon's former hatchet man, and a host of others who made a significant impact for the Gospel, the Church, missions and evangelism during this dynamic period.

I have always been grateful for the ministry of evangelist Luis Palau. Early in this decade Luis invited me to become a member of his Evangelistic Crusade ministry. I enjoyed meeting with his board on several occasions prior to my leaving it because of the pressures of my schedule and responsibilities. While I was on the board I visited with Luis and shared in one of his crusades in London at one of the city's large auditoriums. As has been true with all of Luis' meetings, scores of people that night responded to the Gospel invitation. To this day, Luis remains a deeply-appreciated friend whose influence continues to grow across the world.

On two different occasions, during these years, Pat Robertson, the founder of the Christian Broadcasting Network (CBN), invited me to be a guest on his popular *700 Club* program. The first time was to discuss World Vision's involvement in the Cambodian crisis and our offer of aid to that government with its millions of suffering people due to the war. The second time it was a more general discussion and dialogue concerning the state of Evangelicalism in our nation. Sharing this second program with me was Bill Hybels, pastor of the giant Willow Creek Community Church outside Chicago, which was just then coming into national recognition.

The 1980s marked the growth of Jerry Falwell's Moral Majority, with 250,000 people receiving the newsletter, including over 70,000 pastors. It was also during this time that the scandals surrounding some of our televangelists erupted—including the moral problems with Jim Bakker at PTL and Jimmy Swaggert and his radio/television ministry. As a result of the high profile of these events, my colleagues at Word Books asked if I would write a book for them on the theme of integrity. My friend Bob Larson worked with me on this project and within six months we had a manuscript in hand which was published by Word. This book seemingly had a salutary effect and went into several editions.

Millard Fuller, the founder of the excellent ministry known as Habitat for Humanity, became a friend and invited me to meet, along with some other special friends, with former President Jimmy Carter in Carter's Atlanta office. Millard was seeking counsel regarding the launching of a particular large-scale funding program and graciously invited me to be a part of that strategy meeting. Included in the consultation was the former ambassador to the United Nations and the then mayor of Atlanta, the honorable Andrew Young.

As we spent the day together, the president was most gracious and warm, calling us each by our first name (although of course, we addressed him as "Mr. President"). It was interesting to note that on his large desk in the office was only one item—and that was his Bible.

Habitant for Humanity has had a most significant ministry of building homes at minimal cost for low income families all across the nation as well as in other parts of the world, all of which is done in the name of Christ.

During this period I was first introduced to Rosey Greer, who had been a famed professional football player with the Los Angeles Rams. When I first met him, he had been recently converted and wanted desperately to serve the Lord, to witness—and later become an ordained minister. My counsel to him on an early luncheon engagement that we had together was that he should wait a year or two before he went public with his testimony, being the prominent, widely-recognized personality that he was. I said, "Lay low for awhile and let the Lord build into your life what he wants you to have before you go public in a lot of meetings."

Later, at another time, he indicated to me that he felt this was some of the best advice he had ever received. He has, over the years, become a strong witness for Christ and keenly interested in ministering to inner-city youth.

One day in the middle of this decade, I had a surprise phone call from Billy Graham. He said that he was going to be in San Francisco in two or three days, on his way to some engagements in Seattle, and he wondered if I could possibly come up to San Francisco to spend a day with him at his hotel. Of course I said I would drop everything in order to spend time with him!

Billy, and his colleague and my friend T.W. Wilson, had adjoining rooms at the Hilton Hotel at the San Francisco Airport. I arrived mid-morning and joined him as he was sunning himself around the pool. Billy indicated that he simply wanted to spend time with me and talk about people in the evangelical world, and flattered me by saying he wanted to seek my input regarding the various ministries concerning which he felt I had an understanding. It was a wonderful experience for me to spend the day alone with this choice servant of the Lord.

At noon the three of us went out for lunch and Billy put on dark glasses and a baseball cap so that he would not be recognized. However, as soon as he began to speak in the restaurant people recognized his voice and came over to get his autograph. At the close of the day he suggested that we spend some time in prayer and immediately he fell on his knees alongside his bed and began to pray earnestly for all of the concerns that we had been discussing together that day. It was a truly wonderful moment in my experience, never to be forgotten.

As mentioned in an earlier chapter, I began a very warm friendship with Pat Zondervan when I started my career working with the Zondervan Corporation in 1940. During the decade of the 80s, following the death of his brother Bernie, Pat sold his stock in the publicly-held company to the giant RCA Corporation, which in turn sold its rights to the Harper-Collins Company. Over the succeeding years, Pat and Mary have been among our closest friends. Following the sale of the business they moved to Boca Raton, Florida, where Dorothy and I frequently shared in fellowship with them.

Pat suffered a fatal stroke toward the end of the 80s and Mary asked if I would conduct his memorial service at the Boca Raton Bible Conference Center, which I gladly consented to do. It was indeed a triumphant service for one of God's choice servants.

All of my life I have had a keen interest in both playing golf and following the Professional Golfers Association Tour. (More about that, particularly the special Bible study ministry with the Christian Professional Golfers, in the next chapter.) In the mid 80s, my good friend, PGA golf professional Jim Hiskey, invited me to share in a Christian golfer's retreat at the famed Augusta National golf course in Georgia, home of the annual Master's Golf Tournament. This beautiful course is, along with St. Andrew's in Scotland and Pebble Beach in California, among the most famous in the world.

About twenty of us Christians who enjoy golf spent two days playing the course, sleeping and eating in the famed clubhouse originally developed by golfer Bobby Jones. Dick Halverson, then pastoring the Fourth Presbyterian Church in Washington, was our Bible teacher for the forty-eight hour conference. And, each day we played eighteen holes of golf in our friendly golf competition. My golf score was not all that great, but the experience of playing Augusta, with all the azaleas, flower-lined fairways, great oak trees and all, was unforgettable.

I have also been an avid baseball fan, and it was special to have the star Los Angeles Dodger pitcher Orel Hershiser, along with his wife and family, become part of our Lake Avenue Church congregation. Nineteen ninety-eight was a banner year for Orel, when he broke a number of records, received the Cy Young Award, and was a key factor in the Dodgers winning the World Series that year. I had the pleasure of playing golf with him and striking up an acquaintance with this outstanding Christian athlete.

One of my very special friends is Don Scott, who has served the Lord with distinction in many arenas—including being the Director of our WV work in Laos, then later in Vietnam, the Philippines and in Central America. During this period of time he was named president of World Vision Canada. It has been a joy to visit with Don and his lovely wife Nola in various parts of the world and to share in ministry with him. Early on in his leadership in the Canada program, he invited me to take a jaunt across the Dominion from Vancouver to the Maritimes. We visited cities all along the way to conduct leadership seminars, share in sponsor dinners and to preach in churches in such places as Saskatoon, Winnipeg, Hamilton, Toronto and in New Brunswick. It proved to be a most profitable and enjoyable experience to meet with these Canadian friends of World Vision and to build relationships for the ministry that Don has headed all across Canada.

One of the truly outstanding contributions to the proclamation of the Gospel across the world was a production of the *Jesus* film by Campus Crusade for Christ, a program directed by Paul Eshleman. Over the years this film has been translated into literally hundreds of languages and dialects and has been viewed by literally hundreds of millions of people across the world. My association and friendship with Paul goes back to his high school days in Boca Raton, Florida, where his father was the head of the Bible Town Conference Center in that Florida community. It has been fascinating to note his ever-increasing influence in our evangelical world over these succeeding years.

I had a number of books published during this decade of the 80s, from various publishing houses. Included were *Welcome to the Rest of Your Life*, *Making the Right Choices*, *Boardroom Confidence* (with Bobb Biehl), *Hunger in the Heart of God*, *High Performance* (thirty-one selected chapters from previously published books), *The Fine Art of Friendship* and *The Fine Art of Mentoring*.

The famous Forest Lawn cemeteries in Southern California (four or five of them) every year have a special early morning Easter Sunrise service in their parks. For four years running I was asked to give the Resurrection message at each of these sites which was a special delight and privilege for me. The attendance at each averaged between 1,500 and 2,000 early Resurrection morning worshippers.

Among the awards I gratefully received was one from the Freedom Foundation, in 1986, which was identified as an Individual Achievement Award. Special recognition was given in their publications and in their national conference, as well as a lovely plaque to be hung in my study.

Following my resignation as President of World Vision in 1987, the board named a search committee for my successor, on which committee I was privileged to serve. After a diligent search over several months, reviewing and interviewing a host of candidates, the committee recommended the name of Dr. Robert A. Seiple, President of Eastern College, and the board unanimously invited him to be our fourth president. In the course of our search we asked many leaders in the evangelical world for their recommendations and, among others, our friend Chuck Colson told us, "There is one man above all others whom I would recommend. And that is Bob Seiple!"

This proved to be a wise choice, and I could not have been happier with it. Over the years Bob became a special friend and I was so grateful for the smooth way in which we handled the transition from my leadership to his.

For six months Bob commuted from his role at Eastern College to California on practically a monthly basis so that he could meet the staff and we could have an overlapping of our responsibilities. In my judgment it was a textbook example of how a transition should be handled, smoothly and effectively.

The members of the WV U.S. board asked me to continue on as an honorary member, as did those on the board of World Vision International. Over the succeeding years it was a delight and joy to have continued fellowship with my World Vision colleagues. Even though I did not continue to have voting rights, as an honorary member I was welcomed to the meetings and urged to enter into the discussions and dialogue. And, they asked that I wear the title President Emeritus.

Without question, one of my birthdays during the 80s, on March 1, 1983, was the most memorable and significant night of this decade for me. Earlier on Dorothy and I were told to hold that Friday night and Saturday open and be prepared for a surprise. "Pack your suitcases for overnight", they said, "and don't ask any other questions!" Late that March 1, we were picked up by our friends Jean and Evon Hedley and driven to the Los Angeles Hilton Hotel.

The next day the *Los Angeles Times* reported that the violent weather the previous day and night was the "worst storm of the century," and that a tornado damaged the roof of the Los Angeles Convention Center nearby. Nevertheless, we were ushered into a lovely reception area where, much to our surprise and delight, about 75 or 100 of our friends were gathered for hors d'oeuvres, coffee and punch—and wonderful fellowship. I was amazed and surprised to see friends of ours from across the nation and even elsewhere across the globe. After an hour or so I began to notice that these friends were drifting out of the reception area and wondered where they were going. Presently there were only a half dozen of us left in the room.

We were then told, "Follow us." We did so, being escorted through the hotel kitchen into an amazing sight. There were almost 500 special guests gathered in the Pacific Ballroom. As we walked in, the full orchestra directed by my friend Ralph Carmichael began to play "Happy Birthday" as 500 candles were lit! It was an absolutely unforgettable occasion. The popular television, radio and movie personality, Art Linkletter, whom I had met on numerous occasions previously, was the wonderful master of ceremonies for the event.

Across the back of the head table was a greatly enlarged photograph of me and the slogan "Ted Engstrom—Man in the

Arena." I was absolutely amazed at the hosts of friends who were present and the undeserved remarks that they made in the course of the beautiful dinner. Among those who paid tribute were my mentor, Bob Cook, president of King's College; Bill Bright, president of Campus Crusade for Christ; my friend Jim Dobson, my pastor Paul Cedar, my first employer, Pat Zondervan; Sam Wolgemuth, pastor Gary Demarest, my colleague Larry Ward, my spiritual proteges Herb and Betty Hawkins and my Barnabas, Carlton Booth.

I couldn't stop to enjoy the delicious dinner, but wandered throughout the ballroom greeting these precious friends. With me at the head table were our children and their spouses, Gordon and Lynn, Don and Laurie, JoAnn and Mike. Christian actress and soloist, and my friend, Carol Lawrence, was the special soloist for the evening. She sang several songs as a tribute. The Carmichael Orchestra played some of my favorite gospel songs and choruses—echoing back to my Youth for Christ days.

Additional friends were present from out of the city including my buddy Jack Sonneveldt and his wife Carol from Grand Rapids, Jay Kesler from Wheaton, and particularly my special Chinese friend David Wong, who flew all the way for the event from Hong Kong! I will be eternally grateful to Russ Reid, and his company, for sponsoring this memorable, unforgettable occasion. Let me indicate what I said, in part, in expressing my appreciation to that wonderful group of friends at the close of the banquet. I said, "I accept your love with all of my heart. But in turn—you must hear me now—I want to place all of this now, and again some other day, at the feet of Jesus. I accept your love and am very deeply grateful. But in turn, I transfer this to the One whom I love above all others, our blessed Savior, the Lord Jesus Christ.

"And I want to tell you...that the greatest gift I have apart from the saving grace of the Lord Jesus and His salvation, is this beautiful lady. What a fantastic lady she is. Dorothy is God's gift to me.

"God has proved His faithfulness and has instructed and taught me and led me. I give the praise and glory to Him."

In writing of this event in his much-appreciated biography of me, Bob Owen, formerly editor of our *World Vision* magazine, wrote, "Scores of familiar faces streamed through the Hilton's lobby and made their way to the Pacific Ballroom—businessmen, pastors, college, university and seminary presidents, lawmakers, heads of corporations, entertainment celebrities, journalists and publishers, radio and T.V. executives, white, black, brown—orientals, occidentals, Hispanics, theologians and philosophers.

The affluent, the average, the poor. He had been a friend to them all alike." What an unmerited tribute—but evidence of God's marvelous grace.

"...there are great signs of hope in the spread of God's Kingdom, as the Church continues to look for Christ's early return, in "power and great glory", which is our "blessed hope."

6

REFLECTIONS

The 1990s – The 20th Century's
Closing Decade

THERE WERE A NUMBER OF SIGNIFICANT EVENTS AND
highlights in the early part of this decade, including the 1990
Iraqi invasion of Kuwait and the U.S. launching of Operation
Desert Storm. Iraq was militarily defeated but the strong man,
Saddam Hussein, remained in power, creating a nuisance for the
remainder of this decade.

In 1991, Clarence Thomas was confirmed by the U.S. Senate
as the second African American to sit on the Supreme Court—
although his confirmation was delayed for several months. At
the same time racial tensions were exacerbated as four Los
Angeles policemen were indicted for the videotaped beating of
black motorist Rodney King.

Early in 1992 President George Bush and Russian President
Boris Yeltsin issued a remarkable, historic joint statement officially ending the Cold War. In the same year Bill Clinton became
our U.S. president.

Early in this decade there was a growing awareness of the suffering of Christians in China, Sudan, Vietnam and elsewhere. Much prayer was engendered for the persecuted Church across the world with literally millions of believers martyred for their faith.

It was during this decade that the New Age Movement increased in its impact and influence across the nation. It was attractive because it claimed to bring together the wisdom of the past (the insights of Eastern gurus) and modern science. New Agers redefined God as impersonal energy. Also, the promise of a unified approach to knowledge became an exciting challenge for those who were working on the frontiers of knowledge. To many seekers this was a refreshing breeze that promised fulfillment at all levels without the need of moral restraints or the acknowledgment of sin.

However, these promises turned out to be not merely false, but destructive, for the techniques of the movement are in reality nothing more than the selling of the occult, the popularization of ancient demonism made palatable to the American public. The New Age movement is simply satanism with a benevolent face.

Compassionate and biblical responses to homosexuality and abortion will continue to be needed by the conservative evangelical population at the close of this century. In addition, scandals in the White House will likely continue to occupy great chunks of space and time in our press and electronic media, as we conclude this decade.

As we as a nation and Church have headed into the new millennium, the challenges for us as believers move at an ever-increasing rate—highlighted by the moral deterioration of our government, the increase of drug trafficking, materialism, and assaults on family life. It makes one fear for the future of our children and grandchildren in the days ahead. But there are great signs of hope in the spread of God's Kingdom, as the Church continues to look for Christ's early return, in "power and great glory", which is our "blessed hope."

As I write this final chapter, I've included some more contemporary observations, followed by some brief reflections. Looking back on the previous five decades, my heart rejoices in all the evidence of God's deeply appreciated guidance and direction along the way. "Ebenezer, hither to has the Lord led us." We need not fear the future. This last tumultuous decade has proved to be as equally exciting as the previous five. During this decade I personally no longer have had specific leadership responsibilities but have had the opportunity to do a host of things I had hoped to be able to do—giving quality time to consulting with evangelical leaders and agencies, handling some writing projects, serving on meaningful ministry boards, reflecting on life and having redemptive time with Dorothy, our children and grandchildren.

Without doubt what we as Christians will be facing in the next decade, beginning the third millennium, will be vastly different from today. Billionaire Bill Gates of Microsoft has written, "There will never be a time when there's less change in our lives than there is today." So just imagine what it is going to be like in the twenty first century!

Our response to the rapid pace of change will determine how effective we and our ministries will be in proclaiming the Gospel. It will be fascinating to be a part of the body of Christ as it wrestles with its role in the days that lie ahead, as our Lord may tarry His return.

As I write this last chapter we are presently experiencing dramatic challenges related to the Year 2000 (Y2K) computer problems and glitches. As you may read this chapter, we will be into the new century and it will be most interesting to observe how we have handled this challenge as individuals, in the business arena, in government and across the globe.

It is obviously impossible to have a historic perspective on the 1990s. However, moving into the new century and millennium we can have confidence that the God of history who has moved over the millennia has the future well in control! "Our times are in His hands."

It was during the 90s that we began to note that the majority of evangelicals are not in the Western world. Of the 780 million evangelicals in the world, seventy percent presently live outside of the West. This has proved to have broad implications for world evangelization, as these millions of evangelicals have sought new ways to share the Good News among the unreached poor, most of whom live in Asia.

During this last decade of the twentieth century there have been more Christian prayer movements in the U.S. than in any previous period. A decade or so ago organizations whose primary focus was prayer mobilization for world evangelization were scarce. Presently thousands of people are positioning themselves to intercede for the renewal of Christ's Church and revival in our nation. Seemingly these revival movements focus on world evangelization and not just on revival in our own churches or the restoration of our nation's former glory.

In the midst of a rapidly changing society, accelerating year by year, we need to remind ourselves that there are some things that don't change—such as the essential message of the Gospel committed to us, nor of God Himself, nor the nature of the human heart and certainly not the Commission of Christ to "Go into all the world and preach the Good News to all creation." (Mark 16:15). Hopefully, effective evangelism in the twenty-first century will rediscover the full biblical message and will mobilize the whole Church, express a willingness to explore new methods and new fields and certainly will require total and unconditional dependence upon God.

Billy Graham has stated that in this decade reconciliation has been the number one issue facing the Church. One of the great signs of hope, it seems to me, is that racial reconciliation has become an issue on the front burner for us as evangelicals. For too long it has been delegated simply to talk while remaining very short on action. It seems that many of us who are white Americans now realize the vital need we have to repent of attitudes, superiority and racist actions. We have come to realize that we cannot divorce grace from justice for all of God's children.

———— ———— ————

One of the serious and disturbing problems of the 1990s has been the homeless in our major American cities. The rescue missions of our communities have had a history of over 100 years of involvement, but in these days at the close of the century the problem with homelessness, bag ladies, and displaced people has become most acute, and more must be done to demonstrate Christian compassion. Interestingly, I found myself being invited to meet with a number of these City Rescue Mission leaders in a two-day consulting experience. The first of these was in Seattle with Steve Burger, who later became the president of the International Union of Gospel Missions. I was able to share as well in places like Evansville, Indiana; Denver; Lancaster, Pennsylvania; Akron, Ohio; the two major missions in the Los Angeles area and in several other places, including two separate occasions with the Detroit Rescue Mission headed by my very special friend Don DeVos. The Lord seems to have raised up these specific ministries to meet a crisis need with the downtrodden and disenfranchised of our communities. I salute the ministry of the rescue missions!

Another one of my joys of the 90s has been the opportunity and privilege, as I've retired from active parachurch ministries leadership, to serve on the boards of a number of evangelical agencies and ministries. "Boardmanship" has been a delight to me. I've enjoyed so very much serving on various ministry boards such as Focus on the Family, African Enterprise, The International School of Theology, The English Language Institute for China, Continental Singers, The Orval Butcher Ministries, The Asia Center for Theological Studies, the two World Vision boards—U.S. and International—Azusa Pacific University, Taylor University, George Fox College, Winona Lake Christian Assembly, Maranatha Bible Conference—and of course, my own local Lake Avenue Congregational Church.

As a result of these involvements over the past decades, I have sought to make a study of what Christian "boardmanship" really means and have published two books as a result of these studies. The first, written in collaboration with my friend Bobb Biehl, was *Boardroom Confidence* and the second, written in collaboration with Dr. Bob Andringa, President of the Coalition for Christian Colleges and Universities, entitled *The Nonprofit Board Answer Book*. Both volumes have sold well and seemingly have had a significant impact upon those who render board service. In addition, I've had the delight of turning over the "CEO

Dialogues" which I instituted to Dr. Andringa and John Pearson, CEO of the Christian Management Association. It has been a privilege to continue to serve as Chairman of the Board of this ongoing specialized ministry to leaders of Evangelical agencies and organizations.

Among the many consulting opportunities I have had during this period of time, it was a special delight to consult with the leadership of my friend Chuck Colson's Prison Fellowship. At the time Al Quie, former U.S. Representative from Minnesota and later governor of the state, was the CEO and it was a privilege to work with him and Chuck in evaluating the outstanding ministries emanating from their Washington, D.C. headquarters. Over these 25 years since Colson's imprisonment and conversion, he and his colleagues have made a tremendous impact upon the federal and state prison systems and have ministered to literally hundreds of thousands of prison inmates, not only across America, but in many parts of the world.

Early in 1990 I was chairing the board of trustees at Azusa Pacific University. During this period their president, Dr. Paul Sage, resigned his post and I was asked by the board if I would serve as the acting or interim president while we conducted the search for a new leader.

This was a meaningful nine or ten month period for me as I spent time on the APU campus, working with the senior staff and some of the faculty, as well as identifying with the splendid student body. It was a most enjoyable experience following the pressures of the leadership of World Vision. During this time the APU board invited my friend Dr. Richard Felix, president of Friends University in Wichita, Kansas, to be our new president. Working with him during this decade has been an utter delight. I continued to serve on the board of trustees. In 1995 my colleagues on the board asked me to once again take up the role as chairman. This group of twenty-four committed and godly men and women have given policy direction to the university over these years. It has been a great delight and joy to work with these special individuals who have become, over the years, very meaningful friends.

One of the delightful surprises for us during this time was the announcement that a new student residence hall on the campus of Azusa Pacific University would be named after Dorothy and me. This new building is called the Ted and Dorothy Engstrom Student Resident Hall. At the time of its opening a special chapel and luncheon was held in our honor. A bit later Dorothy and I hosted an evening fellowship with pizza, ice cream and soft drinks for the 300 students who were the first ones living in the dormitory. It was fun!

———   ———   ———

After being away from the leadership of Youth for Christ for over 30 years, I was awakened at 4 a.m. one morning by a telephone call from Singapore. It was my friend Dick Wynn asking me if I would think and pray about serving as chairman of the Youth for Christ International board with its offices in Singapore. Groggily, I indicated that he would have to talk to me at another time when I was much more wide awake!

Ultimately, I did consent to serve in that role for a period of five years, working closely with the president, Gerry Gallimore from Jamaica. It was a stressful experience for me which included a good bit of travel to board meetings in Asia, Europe and elsewhere. However, it was indeed rewarding to be associated once again with these fine young leaders in the ministry of Youth for Christ International and its programs in more than 100 nations of the world. As I have said to my colleagues in YFC, "Once YFC gets in one's blood, it is there to stay!"

In the middle of this decade, Youth for Christ in South Africa celebrated its fiftieth anniversary and invited me to be their special guest, to speak at their large celebration banquet in Johannesburg and then do some training with their youth leadership in a YFC camp. Those were busy days in sharing management and leadership principles with various groups of leaders in the city, including professional trade associations and with a select group of Christian leaders.

During this visit it was a delight to visit in the home and have fellowship with my beloved South African friend, and outstanding Christian government leader, Dr. Louw Alberts and his wife. With me during all of the activities of the week was my longstanding friend Ted Carr, then director of the YFC program in Southern Africa.

———— ———— ————

Early in this decade Dr. James Dobson asked if I would share in a trip to Africa to explore the possibilities of a Focus on the Family presence in some of the more progressive nations on the continent. Thus it was that Focus Vice president Peb Jackson and his colleague Jim Daly and I visited a number of nations in Africa regarding the Focus ministry. We found a most wide open and heartfelt receptivity in Kenya, Zimbabwe, and most especially in South Africa.

We met with various Christian leaders, radio executives, publishers and others and found an eagerness to have a partnership with Dr. Dobson and the Focus on the Family ministry. To me it was a rewarding experience to travel with my friends and sense the receptivity to this significant ministry in several places across the continent.

———— ———— ————

At the beginning of this decade an Indian colleague and Fuller Seminary graduate who worked with World Vision, George Chavanikamannil (we all called him George Chav) felt led of the Lord to establish a new Bible college in northern India. George invited Dorothy and me to participate in the dedication of the college in Dehra Dun, India, a hundred or so miles north of New Delhi. We flew up in a small single-engine plane, landed on a dirt runway and spent several days in fellowship with the new student body and the small but committed faculty.

It was a marvelous experience to share with friends in the inauguration of this Bible school which over these recent years has grown sizeably and is making a tremendous mark upon the communities in northern India, sending out missionaries/pastors across the area. It has been accredited by the Indian government to offer baccalaureate degrees and George continues to give strong and significant leadership to this excellent program. While he was an employee of World Vision, George was named by his fellow workers as the Employee of the Year as he directed our World Vision phone center with a score or more employees reporting to him.

I'm proud of what God has done with this remarkable young man.

———— ———— ————

One of the fine ministries which wonderfully evolved in the decade of the 1990s is the Christian Management Association. The present leadership of John Pearson (who was preceded by Sylvia Nash) and his fine staff is making a significant impact upon parachurch ministries as well as some of our larger churches. It was my joy to be in on the founding of this particular program and then for several years to serve as its board chairman. Alongside the ECFA (Evangelical Council for Financial Accountability), it has served as a watchdog for the performance of hosts of evangelical ministries. The annually sponsored CMA Management Institutes have made a tremendous impact across the American church scene, in annual conferences held in such places as Miami, Chicago, Los Angeles and Colorado Springs.

Another one of the fine organizations developed in the 90s is the Christian Association of Senior Adults (CASA). In 1998 at their large annual conference held at the First Evangelical Free Church in Fullerton, California, they honored several of us "old timers" with what they called the Heritage of Faithfulness Award. Among those of us who received this special tribute, before an audience of well over 2,000 Christian senior citizens, were Cliff Barrows of the Billy Graham Association; my friend Wilbur Nelson, founder and speaker on the morning radio broadcast *The Morning Chapel Hour*; Phil and Louie Palermo; Dr. Bob Rowman of the Far East Broadcasting Co.; businessman Loren Griset and musician Paul Micholson. It was a delightful experience, much appreciated by all of us awardees. The plaque presented to me read:

"For cheering on the faithful,
encouraging the weary and living

a life that is a stirring testament
to God's sustaining Grace."

About the same time my friends at the Conservative
Christian Congregational Conference (the Four Cs) paid me a
special honor at their annual convention in Minneapolis, pre-
senting me with what they called The Outstanding Layman
Award. I was especially touched by the Four Cs leadership indicating that they had only given this award once before in the
fifty-year history of the Conference. This plaque read:

"For Ted W. Engstrom
Your years of service to the church both here
and around the world
CHURCHMAN 'PAR EXCELLENCE'
LOCAL CHURCH CHAIRMAN & OFFICER
MENTOR & MODEL TO MANY
PROLIFIC AUTHOR & LECTURER
PRESIDENT & C.E.O. OF WORLD VISION INT'L
PRESIDENT OF YOUTH FOR CHRIST INT'L
BOARD MEMBER & ADVISOR TO MANY
CHRISTIAN MINISTRIES
A MAN WHO ALWAYS PRACTICES WHAT HE PREACHES
"WELL DONE THOU GOOD & FAITHFUL SERVANT"
Thank you, "4 C's"! Needless to say,
the award was truly overwhelming.

Not long after the beginning of this decade, my friend, businessman Phil Harmon from Seattle, and I discussed the possibility of sponsoring a father/son retreat somewhere in the
Northwest. Phil had a burden for fathers to more closely relate to
their sons and felt that an extended weekend away together in
some attractive site would be mutually beneficial.

Phil asked if I would serve as co-sponsor of such a series of
events which, of course, I was pleased to do. Two such conferences were held in the middle of the decade in the beautiful San
Juan Islands off the coast of Washington State. In each of these,

thirty-five to forty father/son teams met together, and it proved to be a most meaningful, spiritual experience, enabling the father and son to share a special bonding together. On both occasions I had the delightful privilege of my son, Don, joining me.

In this last decade of the 90s I've had the opportunity and privilege of mentoring several godly young men on a regular basis. We meet together for a breakfast or lunch approximately once a month and they share with me what God is doing in their lives and how He is speaking to them. The conversation is free-flowing—talking about everything from their physical activities, their work responsibilities, family life, their walk with the Lord, and their sexuality. Some of these key men with whom I've had this relationship include Ken Kemp, a successful financial advisor, presently living in North San Diego County; Michael Vessey, the son of our special friends Ned and Bette Vessey, also an investment counselor; and Hayne Raucom, the president and owner of a fine computer servicing organization.

Obviously I learn much in counseling with these fine gentlemen and hope my sharing with them is of help particularly in their walk with the Lord. As a result of this experience, I wrote a book titled *The Fine Art of Mentoring* published by Word Books.

In 1997 I was invited to attend a special event at my alma mater, Taylor University—my induction into the Taylor University Athletic Hall of Fame. I was by no means a great athlete in college, having played four years of rather mediocre baseball and a year of basketball, but seemingly my friends on the campus wanted to make this special induction anyway. Possibly one of the reasons for this honor was my influence when serving as chairman of the Taylor board to bring intercollegiate football to the college. Incidentally, the first football team was coached by my protege and special friend, Coach Don Odle.

Dorothy and I were privileged to be at the induction dinner, and then I was introduced and presented the Hall of Fame plaque at halftime during the Saturday football game.

Over the past 40 years Dr. Leighton Ford has been a friend and colleague. I first learned of him when he was Youth for Christ's youngest rally director at age 15 in his hometown in Canada. During his illustrious career he has served as a staff evangelist with the Billy Graham Evangelistic Association (he is the brother-in-law of Dr. Graham) and as founder and director of the Arrow Program, designed to train and encourage young evangelists.

As part of this two year Arrow training program, Leighton has invested his life in scores of promising young evangelists and has conducted periodic week-long sessions with these young men and women in intensive training programs. It has been my joy to have shared as an instructor in sessions of the Arrow Program both at its headquarters in Charlotte, North Carolina, and in Vancouver, British Columbia. I've also had the delightful privilege of serving with Leighton on the World Vision/U.S. board of directors.

In the fall of 1997 I was invited by my friend Dr. Roger Parrott, president of Belhaven College in Jackson, Mississippi, to bring the opening convocation address to the students, faculty and staff at that fine Presbyterian school. I did not realize that they were going to confer on me another honorary doctorate at that occasion. This degree was new to me—Doctor of Management. Whatever its value, the diploma hangs on my office wall, together with those from Taylor University, Seattle Pacific University, Sterling College and John Brown University.

To me, during these past couple of decades, one of the most significant ministries has been that of the Willow Creek Community Church in suburban Chicago with its over 15,000 members meeting on a large beautiful campus in an auditorium seating over 5,000. Bill Hybels was given the vision by the Lord for this ministry and has watched it develop under his strong leadership. It has been a privilege to have formed a warm friendship with Bill, including serving together on both the board of Focus on the Family for a period of time and more recently with the Board of World Vision/U.S. Bill has made a remarkable mark upon the Christian community in these recent years, not only across the U.S. but in many areas of the world where he has led significant and large leadership seminars for Christian leaders.

Another one of my dear friends over the decades has been Dr. Orval Butcher, who for years was pastor of the large Skyline Wesleyan Church in San Diego. Following his retirement from the church he formed an evangelistic association with special emphasis on missions, counseling with struggling pastors, and a student ministry. Orval asked me to serve on his board with some of his close colleagues, which I agreed to do. The Orval Butcher Ministries is a quiet but effective encouragement to many pastors and missionaries across the globe.

One of the significant ministries which arose in the decade of the 90s was the Promise Keepers men's ministry. This program was initiated by the popular Colorado University football coach, Bill McCartney. PK sponsors annually eight or ten large all-men full day rallies—generally Friday night and all day Saturday—in large stadiums across the nation. As many as 60,000 to 70,000 men attended these very special events, challenging them to be godly fathers, husbands and followers of the Lord Jesus. It has been an exciting experience to witness this program develop all across the nation.

In 1997 an estimated million men met on the Mall near the Potomic River in Washington, D.C. for a full day's testimony to the power of the Gospel operative in the lives of these men. For those in attendance it was an unforgettable experience.

———

One of the personal joys for Dorothy and me over the past six decades has been an active participation in our local church, the last three and a half decades of which were involved in our home church in Pasadena—Lake Avenue Congregational Church. In these years I have filled just about every leadership role in the church including church moderator/chairman, trustee, deacon—and teacher of a senior adult Bible class.

During this time I have served with three dear pastors, Ray Ortlund, Paul Cedar and Gordon Kirk. Each of these choice servants have been very close friends. I have had a longstanding policy as far as my priorities are concerned: first, my relationship with God and with the Lord Jesus; secondly, my relationship with Dorothy and my family; thirdly, my responsibility as a churchman; and finally, my career path. I have not always held as closely to these priorities as I should have, but have felt that they are vitally important for me as a Christian leader.

I have earnestly felt that there needs to be lines of responsibility and accountability that I have and receive as a leader. First, I have often indicated that every Christian leader needs to have a Barnabas, "Son of Encouragement" in his life. The Apostle Paul had his friend Barnabas who shared with him in ministry following the apostle's three years in the wilderness. Early in the book of Acts we read that Barnabas and Paul went hither and yon; later it was Paul and Barnabas serving together. Barnabas was indeed the prayer partner and counselor for the apostle.

For me, this person was my dear friend Dr. F. Carlton Booth, to whom I have referred earlier in this book. Carlton had an office near mine prior to his death a few years back and was always available for counsel, prayer and spiritual guidance. I would go to him often to share challenges and his wise counsel was always deeply appreciated. He was my Barnabas.

Second, I have felt that every leader needs to have a Timothy or Timothys. The Apostle Paul had his son in the faith to whom he wrote two magnificent letters of guidance and instruction. I'm certain that Paul and Timothy learned from each other; it was a beautiful relationship. God has allowed me to have numerous "Timothys" over these past decades for whom I am most grateful.

Third, Paul had a very special friend of whom he writes in his Philippian letter—Epaphroditus. This man was a close confidant and "fellow soldier" with the apostle. They were quite evidently buddies. I have thoroughly enjoyed this type of relationship with peers such as my very special friends, Evon Hedley and Jack Sonneveldt.

Fourth, I have long since felt that every leader needs to be part of an accountability group. I learned about this type of experience many years ago from pastor Ray Stedman in Palo Alto and the experience he had with godly laymen who surrounded him. Years back I suggested such an arrangement to Ray Ortlund, indicating that we might form such a group. Ray was heartily in favor of it and now, thirty years later, such a group still exists of which I have been a part all of these years.

One of the joys that Dorothy and I have appreciated over the past decades has been spending vacation and holiday time on ocean cruises. We have had more than twenty such cruises, early on traveling with our friends Pat and Mary Zondervan and later with Evon and Jean Hedley and Dwight and Audrey Swanson, friends in the Palm Desert area where we have our condominium.

These cruises included a number of trips through the inner passage to Alaska, several times in the Caribbean and through the Panama Canal, a most delightful trip up the Norwegian coast to the ice-bound island of Spitzenberg, down the Danube River from Munich to Budapest and a very special cruise which I hosted for some of our Azusa Pacific University donors to the Greek Islands and the Holy Land.

All of these events were memorable and most appreciated by the two of us—for relaxation, no phones, conferences and daily activities—and times to be enjoyed together. We have taken these to be wonderful gifts from the Lord for us to enjoy. Another one of the joys that Dorothy and I have experienced over the years has been our condominium in Palm Desert, California on the Monterey Golf Course. For many years I enjoyed playing golf with special friends who had homes on the course.

One particular friend there, Bill Bone, is the largest resort developer in the area, had arranged for a special price to be offered to us for our unit, which of course we deeply appreciated. We have enjoyed so much getting away on occasion to this special place for retreat and relaxation. I mentioned earlier my interest in golf and professional golfers. Early in the decade my friend, golf professional Jim Hiskey, asked me to lead a Bible study with the Christian golfers on tour at the annual Bob Hope Golf Classic in Palm Springs. This I was pleased to do and for several years led the Wednesday evening Bible study, which occurs at all of the tour events annually.

With this I have had the delight of making the acquaintance of a number of golf professionals who attended the sessions, including such well–known pros as Steve Jones, Scott Simpson, Corey Paven, David Ogrin, Bernhard Langer, Larry Mize, Paul Stamkouski, Loren Roberts and Morris Hatalsky.

Earlier, during a visit to South Africa, I was privileged to attend a reception held at the home of Gary Player, noted South African professional golfer, which he hosted for Billy Graham who was conducting a series of evangelistic rallies during that time. The Gary Player ranch, just outside of Johannesburg, is a delightful place which includes a tennis court, a golf green and two full length golf holes.

All through the years I have been grateful that God has given me health and strength for all of my travels and responsibilities. It includes well over 100 overseas trips, 136 countries, and millions of miles by air. Through it all, the Lord has provided protection (with only a few frightening incidences in the air travel).

There have been only three times in these past six decades when I have been seriously ill (not including the month in Massachusetts for the hip replacement). Once, in Brazil, I was desperately ill in a Sao Paulo hotel room until finally, after five or six days, my missionary friend Jim Savage brought in a local doctor who gave me medicine tasting like rubber which almost overnight cured my stomach illness.

A second time, while in a pastor's conference in India with Sam Kamaleson, I again was ill and a doctor there ordered me home as rapidly as possible. In order to get home, I had to fly first of all to New Delhi, overnight in a hotel there, fly on to Hong Kong, change planes to get as far as Honolulu, where again a doctor put me in a local hospital—a ward with eight or ten other patients! Dorothy came from home to be with me there for the remaining days that I was hospitalized.

Late in 1997 I felt drained of all energy, was suffering severe back and leg pains and after a month or two of chiropractic treatments, acupuncture and visits to the doctor, my doctor friend, Richard Davis, put me in the Arcadia Methodist Hospital for six days. I did not realize it at the time but the Lord had a purpose for my being on my back and out of circulation for that period of time. He ministered to me in a very special way day by day with the wonderful meaning of His marvelous grace. I shared my thoughts with the many visitors who came by to see me and we together rejoiced in the wonderful truth of God's marvelous grace.

During the time that I was hospitalized, my special friend, colleague and accountability group member, Gordon Johnson, lying in a room across the hall from my hospital room, went to be with the Lord. It was a shock to realize that this dear friend, so close by, went on to his rich reward.

Thus, I thank God for good health, recognizing that my two predecessors as president of World Vision both died—in my judgment prematurely—because of diseases picked up through their overseas travels.

During these past three and a half decades of leadership in World Vision I have been most blessed by having wonderfully competent and efficient secretarial support, beginning with my former secretary from YFC days, Lorrayne Edburg, now in heaven, Denise Schubert and Mary Soop, who served me for a number of years, and for the past dozen or more years Polly Berry. These beautiful, committed ladies have been of inestimable help to me in my responsibilities.

In addition, two men have served as administrative assistants and have proved to be wonderful gentlemen with servant hearts. The first was John Foulkes and the second was George Marhad, who has assisted me so meaningfully in giving me background material for this book and has over the years supplied such helpful background material for my writing, addresses and various responsibilities. To these friends I am deeply grateful.

As Dorothy and I reflect over these past fifty–nine years together we are extremely grateful for God's gift to us of three wonderful children, all of them adopted as infants, who have warmed, blessed and enriched our lives over the years. They have brought us five great grandchildren and now, at the end of this decade, two lovely little great-grandsons.

We consider these adopted children of ours, now mature adult parents, to be one of God's great gifts to us as husband and wife.

Early on in my Christian experience, as a young believer, God gave me my life verse, which is Psalm 32:8: "I will instruct you and teach you in the way you should go; I will counsel you with My eye upon you." At the close of this chapter let me testify that God has proved to me over and again that His Word is sure. He has indeed, in innumerable ways and in a host of varied circumstances, proved this verse true in my life. He has led and guided me in wonderful ways, even though oftentimes against a temporary rebellious spirit. I thank Him for allowing me to rest in full assurance on this beautiful promise.

I have used this promise on literally thousands of occasions in signing books, Bibles, letters and in other ways—trusting it would be a blessing to those who would check the reference. In light of all that I've experienced over these past six decades of service, I look at the question the Apostle Peter asked in his second epistle, "What kind of people are we to be?" He answers his own rhetorical question saying, "We ought to be people who live holy and godly lives." This is what I have wanted for my life as I look forward to the greatest sign of hope—the day of Christ's return.

As I have sought to do in this book, it is important to remember certain things from our past so that we connect with the purposes of God which continue from the past all the way into the bright future when Christ returns—remembering the Lord our God, His ways, His Kingdom, His coming, and His righteousness, His will for the unsaved coming from every tribe, race, ethnic group, language—and His desire for the gates of hell not to prevail against His Kingdom. God continues His search world-wide for men and women to stand in the gap and build up the wall of righteousness in people's lives and in society.

In the previous chapters I have sought to review my personal perspective and memories of only a fragment of the body of Christ who are commonly called evangelicals. I have had the privilege of knowing literally thousands of evangelical leaders and colleagues over my sixty-plus years of ministry, and have tried to highlight many of their lives and activities.

Since my early remembrances during the depression years and the sacrificial and momentous World War II years, evangel-icals have shared a sense of destiny and call to reach their gener-ation with the Gospel of Christ and communicate His love in practical ways. The essence of this call has been reconfirmed in my opinion in each decade, though the forms and expressions, in both the church and parachurch organizations. I have usually changed to adapt to contemporary needs and aspirations.

As I look to the next century and a new millennium, I am optimistic that the role and call of evangelicals will continue to find fresh applications and expressions, while struggling to stay faithful to our essential purpose. Perhaps the parable of the weeds and wheat in Matthew 13:24-30, is an apt description of the environment in which we will increasingly minister in the future. It cautions us that weeds of destruction have been sown among the growing wheat harvest of new and maturing believ-ers. The owner of the field says to let both grow together until the harvest, so as not to damage the wheat.

We can easily be discouraged if we choose to focus only on the fast-growing weeds all around us (and often highlighted in the mass media), and miss the amazing reality that an unprece-dented harvest is being gathered by the Lord of the Harvest for His kingdom and for eternal life. Let me illustrate a few exam-ples of where that harvest seems to show great promise.

There seems to be an amazing movement worldwide in the body of Christ and even in parts of general society toward repen-tance and reconciliation. Primarily it seems that Christ has accel-erated His determination to purify His Church by requiring His Body to start dealing more intensively with past corporate and personal sins. We see this in the budding attempts at racial rec-onciliation in the Promise Keepers movement, in the Truth and

Reconciliation movement in South Africa, and in a variety of church-wide efforts to begin repentance for historical evils such as the Crusades, the holocaust silence, tribal massacres, and other corporate sins. On the family and personal front, marriages and inter-personal conflicts are being healed as repentance and reconciliation are being sincerely expressed and fruits of repentance are being demonstrated.

There is also evidence of a growing youth movement to seek purity of life and to learn how to live sacrificially and to reach a lost and hurting generation with the Gospel of Christ. As one who gave literally decades of my life to helping youth find and follow Christ, I am heartened by this movement. Whether it is the nearly one million youth involved annually in a Thirty Hour Famine in their churches to focus on world hunger and pray for the lost, or the stadiums throughout America packed with teenagers who make vows of sexual abstinence until marriage, or the nearly 20,000 Urbana University students who gather to seriously consider the call of world evangelization on their lives and work, we have a new generation of youth and young adults willing to live biblically moral lives and to serve Christ and humanity sacrificially.

Within a large number of our churches, I am also heartened by the deep trust in the Holy Spirit that pastors are placing in their lay leaders and congregations. Many of these pastors and church leaders are finding fresh applications of the equipping role outlined in Ephesians 4:11-13, and are expressing confidence in the Holy Spirit to enable lay colleagues in their ministries in neighborhoods, businesses, government, and communities as never before. As one who has always thought of myself as a layman, and who has encouraged lay ministry, I believe this kind of biblical team-building and servant leadership is enhancing a movement of lay ministry envisioned in the I Peter 2 description of a "holy priesthood…a chosen people and royal priesthood."

Related to this, there are also encouraging signs of new cooperation in much of the body of Christ in forming ministry partnerships and strategic alliances. It may be due in part to the growing necessities urged by global population beyond six billion people, and to growing world poverty, and the need for new efficiencies and to reduce redundancies in ministry for the sake of the Christ's kingdom. But as someone who has been heavily involved in Christian corporate and organizational life for over sixty years, I applaud the efforts to join together and combine resources, talents and prayers to communicate Christ, to reach the poor and unreached, to care for children and the needy, and to permeate society as salt and light as never before.

The growing complexities of our world seem also to require a new search for the profound, simple, foundational truths that bring clarity of purpose and hope for the future. Jesus illustrated breaking through complexity to the simple truth in Matthew 22 when He said all the Law and prophets hang on the greatest commandment—to love God and neighbor.

My hope is that the dawn of a new millennium in our mind-boggling, complex world will lead us to re-discover the few truly essential simple truths, and their Author Christ Jesus, that a new generation will need for both quality living and eternal life. I wouldn't be surprised if some of them have something to do with losing one's life to save it, to love God and neighbor as the rule of life, and to seek God's kingdom above all else and trust God to provide for one's needs.

A lifetime of serving Christ and knowing thousands of His choice servants has merely served to deepen my conviction about how unshakable His kingdom is, how true His Word is for practical living, and how faithful God will be to impart a fresh mantle of Spirit-led power, creativity and sacrificial service to a new generation.

God's desire is that when His Son returns to earth He will find a deep, active faith among His Church—people abandoned to the King of the kingdom and deriving their lifelong hope from the imminent return of Christ to earth.

As I come to the conclusion of this book, and of this century—and perhaps close to the end of my life—I have but one prayer. That is, "Lord, let me finish well!"

Reflecting back on these six decades of ministry has been a moving experience for me and I am deeply grateful to God for leading me in the promised "plain paths". God is good. His mercies endure forever. His love is all encompassing. His ways are past finding out. I praise His name! Amen!